On Listening and Learning

Gateways to Counselling

Consultant editor:
Windy Dryden, Professor of Counselling at Goldsmiths College,
University of London

Series editor:
Maria Stasiak

Project manager:
Carron Staplehurst

The *Gateways to Counselling* series comprises books on various aspects of counselling theory and practice. Written with the assistance of the Central School of Counselling and Therapy, one of the largest counselling training organisations in the UK, the books address the needs of both students and tutors and are relevant for a range of training courses, regardless of specific orientation.

Other books in the series include:

STARVING TO LIVE
The paradox of anorexia nervosa
Alessandra Lemma-Wright

**AN INTRODUCTION TO CO-DEPENDENCY FOR
COUNSELLORS**
Gill Reeve

COUNSELLING IN A GENERAL PRACTICE SETTING
James Breese

TRANSCULTURAL COUNSELLING
Zack Eleftheriadou

COUNSELLING SKILLS FOR PROFESSIONAL HELPERS
John Pratt

ON LISTENING AND LEARNING

Student counselling in further and higher education

Colin Lago and Geraldine Shipton

Central Book Publishing Ltd
London

First published 1994
by Central Book Publishing Ltd
Centre House, 56B Hale Lane
London, NW7 3PR

© 1994 Colin Lago and Geraldine Shipton

Typeset in 10 on 12 point Century Roman and Optima by
Intype, London
Printed in Great Britain by
Tudor Printing, Park Road, Barnet

Cover illustration by Helen S. Roper

British Library Cataloguing in Publication Data

Lago, Colin
    On Listening and Learning: Student Counselling
    in Further and Higher Education. – (Gateways to
    Counselling Series)
    I. Title II. Shipton, Geraldine
    III. Series
    378.1946

ISBN 1–898458–25–1

Contents

Acknowledgements

We would like to thank many people for their help and support: Christine Davison, our secretary, whose work has been essential to the project; our clients and colleagues, who have inspired us to write; our partners, for their kind and consistent encouragement; our children Catherine and Matthew Shipton and Rebecca and James Lago for tolerating preoccupied parents; and finally Maria Stasiak, whose editorial skills we have valued greatly.

Introduction

The last few years have seen a flurry of activity in the publication of books about counselling. Some of this upsurge in interest is heartwarming to counsellors who work in colleges and universities and signifies, by association, a recognition that the work they do is worthwhile and remarkable. However, within this rapidly evolving industry, scant attention has been paid to the unique role of counselling in educational settings. This means that 'student counsellors' appear to be slightly off-centre in the counselling world despite being significant in number and, in terms of the impact they make on young people in crisis, potentially well-placed to effect change that can be highly beneficial at a critical juncture in the lives of students. This book hopes to redress the balance a little.

Outside of our frame of reference are some valuable undertakings which may embrace the use of some counselling skills but which do not, in themselves, constitute counselling. Such endeavours include career guidance, advice-giving and advocacy work. Consequently, in this book we will not be discussing how to offer help with the material problems of students, although we know that lack of money is a hugely disabling factor which oppresses and depresses our clientele.

Nor will we look at the grey area that encompasses the efforts of sensitive and sometimes talented educationalists and others to extend their role in the direction of informal counselling or what is sometimes referred to lyrically as pastoral care. This book is about the work of professional counsellors whose core work features the provision of personal counselling to students and staff in higher education.

Our effort to distinguish the work of counsellors from that

of other colleagues in education parallels the way student counselling has struggled over time to delineate itself from other, related activities, as we shall demonstrate in Chapter 1. Some counselling services have sprung out of student welfare or advice services, others have their foundations in student health services while many, including our own, have emerged, rootless as it were, from a need identified by academics, administrators and students themselves. Nowadays most institutes of higher education and many colleges of further education have in place well-established counselling services.

An explanation is perhaps required here to distinguish between the sectors of further and higher education. Further education colleges provide for post-school courses for people aged 16+ wishing to take qualifications beneath degree level. These courses include GCSEs, 'A' levels and technical qualifications for differing occupations. We use the terms institutions of higher education and university interchangeably. These institutions generally teach to degree and higher degree levels and offer research programmes that lead to Masters and Doctorate degrees.

In recent years the overwhelming majority of services have reported an increase in demand on their time by growing numbers of students who are bringing problems or experiences that vary from temporary homesickness or study problems to a whole gamut of psychiatric conditions, emotional trauma and personal disasters. The range of presenting problems is discussed in Chapters 2, 3, 4 and 5 and includes an attempt to locate and identify difficulties not only in individuals themselves but also in the interaction between people and organisations. We have also included a discussion about some ways in which a developmental understanding of the life-cycle can usefully inform a view of the tensions that persuade students to seek counselling.

The expansion in the take-up of counselling in Britain has been discussed in the media. Common causes may include the catalogue of national and international disasters such as the Hillsborough Stadium catastrophe and the sinking of the *Herald of Free Enterprise*, which gained a lot of publicity for the need to follow-up psychological work with the survivors, families and friends of victims. The notion of post-traumatic

Introduction

stress seems to have captured the imagination of journalists, who in turn have helped to make respectable the need for help with other psychological difficulties. Another hypothesis about the expansion of need for counselling is that as the society we live in becomes increasingly mobile socially, the old family and neighbourly networks of support can no longer rally round to help people in trouble, who are then forced to turn to professionals. A Gallup Poll carried out for the Royal College of Psychiatrists in 1992 found that 85 per cent of 2,000 people surveyed believed that depression was caused by life events and that counselling, not drugs, was the appropriate treatment.

Such trends obviously affect students and are partly responsible for the swelling numbers of students seeking counselling. Furthermore, the student population itself has expanded dramatically in size in most institutions, whilst the teaching staff has not increased to the same extent. This means that there is less opportunity for lecturers and administrators to give extra time and attention to helping students who are in difficulty. As counsellors we are pleased to see the apparent recognition of psychological and relationship-based approaches to helping people but we cannot hide from some less palatable implications which are that individual solutions to problems seem to be replacing community-based or political effort to enhance society and that counselling has become 'flavour-of-the-month'. Already certain newspapers have begun to highlight disenchanting stories about counselling practice as if disappointed that the latest craze is not the longed-for cure-all that, of course, counsellors and many of their clients, as well as readers of this book, know it can never be. Student counsellors also tread a thin line in arguing in their institutions for more staff to fulfil an important need while at the same time promoting a realistic expectation of the benefits and limitations of counselling.

Throughout this book we will note the ways in which the educational setting makes student counselling different from counselling carried out in other settings. Some differences are obvious; for example, students are predominantly in college during term-time, when the bulk of counsellors' contact work takes place. Thus, most counselling is shaped by the pattern of ten to twelve-week terms. Colleges of further education have slightly longer terms. Waiting lists, which have become a common feature of student counselling, may mean a student who attends for help halfway through a term may not be able to begin counselling until just before the end of term. Deadlines for academic assignments may then be missed or exams failed, causing concern to both students and counsellors. The constraints of deadlines, exam timetabling and lengths of term uniquely affect student clients and counsellors in a manner that is not generally experienced in the broader counselling field. Crises can occur at any time and do not fit into convenient slots determined by terms.

Another clear difference is the age group from which the majority of students are drawn: this generally spans the developmental stages of late adolescence and early adulthood. Developmental challenges which face young people of this age include: growing towards independence; forming new intimate relationships; establishing a sexual identity; and developing a balance between the need to compete and the need to cooperate with their peers.

In recent years, the traditional picture of young students has shifted to include a substantial number of students from a much wider age range, as exemplified in the popular film *Educating Rita*. These 'mature' students already have life experiences which are akin to those of clients in other adult settings. However, the educational project on which they have embarked means that they have to contend with new academic demands and the effects of transition between their former working lives and their present ones in education.

The need to move 'beyond the counselling room' to do preventative work with the institutions which employ us and the colleagues who work alongside us comprises the focus for Chapters 6, 7 and 8. It is in this area that student counsellors often play a vital and little-publicised role in education. This work can prove exacting, since it demands skills in group-work, committee work, teaching and staff development on top of the essential therapeutic skills!

The areas of work described as preventative and developmental are those which are geared towards ensuring that the overall educational environment does not deliberately cause upset in students' lives simply through its working practices, and that groups of students and staff are aided in the skills development necessary to maximise their own potential within the academic environment. This may involve activities as diverse as running staff training courses for personal tutors, offering stress management seminars to both staff and students, and facilitating study skills workshops. The student counsellor, therefore, has a community work role as well as that of a therapeutic worker with individuals.

Finally, we conclude with some thoughts about future scenarios for counselling services and about competing pressures which seem to be moulding us in this country, both from within our own profession and from the changing needs of educational establishments who engage us.

Part I
THE DEVELOPMENT OF STUDENT COUNSELLING

1

Student Counsellors in Further and Higher Education

Provision, practice and professional issues

HISTORY AND DEVELOPMENT OF STUDENT COUNSELLING

The profession of student counselling has come a long way from the first counsellor training courses in the late 1960s. Historically, there has always been a strong 'pastoral' element in British education. By this it is meant that colleges have long recognised the importance of caring for students as whole people, not just as intellects to be developed. To a certain extent, the very old and distinguished universities (Oxford, Cambridge, Durham) influenced early models of tutoring, where students were afforded the opportunity of working in one-to-one tutorials with their tutors. The legacy of this in present-day practice can be found in the work of tutorial staff offering individual and group tutorials and seminars and in the counselling relationships between student and counsellor.

From quite early on, then, the role of tutor involved responsibilities and aims that went beyond the narrow boundaries of the subject they were teaching. An opportunity existed for students to experience an older person as a role model, a mentor, as someone they could share parts of their life experience with and so on. This aspect of tutorial work became quite a distinguishing feature between the British and continental systems of higher education.

Critics of this system expressed anxieties that, often, tutors were not trained in these wider roles (beyond the pure dissemination of their subject). Some have abused, often unthinkingly and unconsciously, their power over students and generally been patronising in carrying out their tasks.

The newer disciplines of counselling and guidance that had become established during the early decades of this century in the higher education system in the United States began to impact upon the education system in Britain during the mid-1960s. The first American course in counsellor education was offered by Harvard University during the summer session of 1911 (Milner 1974).

These newer disciplines offered theories and models of professional practice that recognised the importance of both the developmental processes through which traditionally aged students (18–23) progress, as well as their need for supportive guidance from adults. In addition, the influence of the psychoanalytic tradition inherited from Europe earlier in the century along with later developments in the field of humanistic psychology in the USA meant that more sophisticated models of psychological and emotional help were becoming increasingly available.

EARLY TRAINING COURSES AND COUNSELLOR APPOINTMENTS

The significance of these various historic strands come together in the coincidental establishment (*circa* 1965–70) of full-time postgraduate counselling courses at universities such as Swansea, Keele, Aston and Reading. Aston and Keele were the first full-time courses offering training for student counsellors.

Theoretical and experienced support for the teaching on these courses was obtained through having visiting Fulbright scholars from the United States. Already eminent as counselling practitioners and trainers in the United States, these academic appointees brought with them invaluable experience and educational know-how that really secured the professional underpinnings of these courses in the early years. Other significant courses that commenced around the same time were those at London University (Department of Extra-Mural Studies) and South-West London College.

In line with the development ten of these courses, some universities and polytechnics made appointments of student counsellors, sometimes linked to careers guidance, accommodation provision and welfare roles.

One significant model of provision that was established at this time was that of the Counselling and Careers Service at Keele University. Headed by Audrey Newsome, this combined student service employed five full-time counsellors who offered both counselling and careers guidance. With her colleagues, Brian Thorne and Keith Wylde, a book was written about their work, *Student Counselling in Practice* (1973). Readers interested in these early days of student counselling are recommended to consult this very readable and influential book.

By the end of 1973, the Association for Student Counselling (which had been created in 1970) had almost 200 members, a reasonable number given the newness of this profession within education.

THE PRESENT POSITION OF STUDENT COUNSELLING

The range of counselling provision today is considerably wider across the further and higher education sector. With the exception of just one or two, all the old universities and the new universities (formerly polytechnics) have counselling services as well as a very considerable number of colleges in the further education and tertiary sector.

In 1992, membership of the Association for Student Counselling stood at 552. Not all student counsellors are members of this Association but this figure does give an indication of the increase in counselling posts over twenty years.

Counsellors are employed on a very wide range of salaries and conditions of service. Colleges also vary considerably in their provision of counselling even when they do compare in terms of similarity of student numbers, courses offered, location and so on! It is not unusual for a counsellor in one college to be available for ten to fifteen hours per week on a part-time basis as a wider part of their teaching post and for other equivalent colleges to have at least two full-time counsellors. Counsellors may also have other welfare roles as part of their employment contracts, e.g. accommodation provision and advice for students, careers advisory work, welfare advice and staff training. Two contrasting examples of counselling services are given below.

The first example is of a counselling service situated in one of the new universities. The first full-time counsellor was appointed in 1972. The institution had an approximate student population of 4,000 at that time and within two years the counsellor's work had increased significantly. As a consequence, a second full-time counsellor was appointed. The two counsellors initiated first-year talks to students, ran a wide range of groups and courses and offered occasional staff development courses in addition, of course, to offering counselling to individual students.

In 1978 a third full-time counsellor was appointed. The provision of three full-time counsellors (paid on academic salaries) meant that a very wide range of appropriate and innovative work was achieved, over the years, in that institution. This work included the publication of a variety of advice, information and study booklets for students and staff and the development of staff and student training.

Appropriately resourced, this team were able to work towards a vision of what a good counselling service can offer an institution. By contrast, the second institution, an FE college, appointed a student counsellor in the early eighties who was responsible for counselling, welfare advice, accommodation, first aid, students with special needs and staff training. The post was paid on a clerical grade and no secretarial/reception cover was given.

In this situation, unfortunately, because of institutional priorities and restraints on spending, there has not been any development at all. The counsellor has had to work out her own ways of surviving an impossible workload without any hope of increased provision or a reduction in the huge variety of tasks she is responsible for. She is charged with a staff training role and yet is paid less than academic staff! Even the individual counselling she undertakes is affected by the very limited time she can offer to any one person. Not having an office budget means that she has to pay for professional consultancy and further training out of her own low salary.

This second scenario, sadly, has been and still is the norm for many student counsellors who are often highly qualified and deeply committed to their work. With increased expansion of student numbers and reduced resourcing of the further and higher education sectors at the present time, our fear is that the situation for student counsellors may become worse.

HOW STUDENT COUNSELLORS WORK: THERAPEUTIC ORIENTATION AND MODELS OF PRACTICE

Student counsellors work in a variety of ways that reflect their own training, the nature of the academic year and the specific conditions in which they work. A cursory overview of counsellors' theoretical orientations was carried out some years ago by the Association for Student Counselling.

In general terms what emerged from this study was that there existed a fairly equal division between those who described themselves as psychodynamic and those who were broadly humanistic. Smaller groups were broadly identified as 'eclectic' and cognitive-behavioural.

One question then that might emerge from the above overview is the degree to which different theoretical models are more effective with this specific client group. Unfortunately, there is no clear evidence of any theoretical approach being better than another when applied to student counselling. Findings emerging from the Psychotherapy Research Unit at Sheffield University indicate that clients are most helped by counsellors who are comfortable with and convinced of their ways of working. Inevitably the personality and communication style of the counsellor will have a major impact both upon individual outcomes for clients as well as upon the wider institution.

THE DEVELOPMENT OF SHORT-TERM WORK

During the last three or four years a considerable amount of counsellor interest has been focused upon the development of models of short-term counselling work. Indeed, student counsellors have run their own one-day conferences to explore these ways of working.

Notwithstanding this current interest, it is important to

realise that long-term counselling work with students has always been a statistically small part of the counsellor's working load. On average, students attend for between three and four sessions. The brevity of the intervention is appropriate, we believe, to the stage of development most young people have reached. They are at a time in life where the exploration of relationships and the striving for independence demand social activity as the arena in which these challenges are explored. However, overall theories of human development do not allow for individual differences of distress and patterns of upbringing. Thus the existence of medium and long-term counselling work for specific individuals is necessary as well.

Medium-term counselling work (e.g. between four and ten sessions of approximately fifty minutes duration) might be engaged in with up to a third of all clients.

The drive to explore models of minimum intervention has stimulated fierce debate between student counsellors. Inevitably, this interchange has been influenced by those counsellors' own theoretical modes and the very real debate as to the questionable value of artificially 'speeding up' the psychological healing process.

Advocates of the short-term approach recognise the limitations of short-term work but certainly do not try simply to condense what they would do over a longer term. Instead they choose to focus on specific elements that seem central to the client's distress and once agreed with the client, concentrate upon these.

Michael Barkham, a research psychologist at Sheffield University, has developed a model of brief work with patients and clients which is focused and effective. This is called the 'two-plus-one' model and is a cognitive-behavioural approach involving two sessions of counselling delivered a week apart and a follow-up session delivered at a later date. It seems that in a substantial number of situations, the initial impact of counselling upon the clients can be considerable and can often be enough to enable more normal functioning to be achieved. The follow-up session some time later is an opportunity to check on progress and hopefully consolidate changes made.

Other focused models include brief psychodynamic counselling and short cognitive analytic therapy, though these two approaches are nowhere near as brief as the two-plus-one model. Indeed, they might span anything between ten and twenty sessions. In general terms, student counsellors are already containing at least 75 per cent of their clients within these parameters.

Any short-term focused work using the above models certainly requires formal training, specialist supervision from within that approach and considerable diagnostic skills combined with clinical experience. Some theorists of short-term work argue that the demands upon counsellors of working in such focused ways are very considerable.

Some student counsellors, as an alternative to working long-term with clients, offer therapy groups which clients may join after an initial period of personal work. The long-term work may therefore be carried out by the counsellor in a group setting where between five and ten students are seen at a time. Though obviously not the same as individual therapy, the group does offer a useful vehicle for clients to develop and a mechanism whereby the counsellor can see more people in the time available.

THE ROLE OF TERMS AND VACATIONS

Education is a sphere in which there is a definite rhythm to work. Terms each have a different 'feel', holidays provide an enforced break and each year tends to work towards a climax of examinations. This makes it imperative that counsellors develop creative ways of working with disruption and transience. Work seems to get speeded up or slowed down by both parties as vacations or exams loom or pass. Although most students will receive short-term counselling some will be seen for much longer periods, commonly for up to an academic year. A much smaller number will be seen for several years by some counsellors, though normally not much longer than the duration of their time at college. In some ways, it can be argued that the pattern of breaks is good preparation and rehearsal for the eventual ending of medium and longer-term work. In any case, all clients are forced to contend with large gaps in continuity caused by vacations. Impermanence and transience are thus integral features of student counselling. It may also be the case that student counsellors, out of necessity, must trust the client to be able to cope with both regular breaks and a certain amount of 'unfinished business' which they may have to postpone investigating to a later stage in life.

THE NEW 'PROFESSIONALS' – HOW DO PEOPLE BECOME STUDENT COUNSELLORS?

Though the question in the above title is very clear and exact, the response below, unfortunately, is far less precise. The career paths of existing student counsellors do not neatly fit simple, linear models of professional development. From conducting an informal review of colleagues the authors discovered a wide range of previous qualifications and disciplines from which present student counsellors have emerged. For example the following disciplines were represented:

1   education: colleagues who had formerly been in this job sector had worked as teachers and lecturers. Often their original teaching discipline (e.g. microbiology or physical education) did not seem in itself to be naturally connected to their later development as counsellors;
2   the ministry: several student counsellors are or have been either ordained ministers of the church or brothers or nuns in a holy order;
3   engineering: several student counsellors were formerly practising engineers.

Other student counsellors have also come from the fields of:

4   youth and community work;
5   social work;
6   nursing;
7   occupational therapy;
8   careers advisory work.

Despite the variety of disciplines and previous positions held by student counsellors, what does seem consistent across all these examples is an underlying concern for the psychological and emotional health of individuals. Student counselling as an occupation has thus enabled many to realise this deep concern for the well-being of others in everyday practice.

Only one example is known to the authors of a student counsellor who followed his first degree in psychology with a postgraduate diploma in counselling and then obtained a position as a student counsellor in a university at the age of 24. The more general tendency is for counsellors to have had a considerable range of previous vocational experience before choosing to specialise in student counselling.

STUDENT COUNSELLORS AND THEIR PROFESSIONAL ASSOCIATION

The professional body that is most pertinent to student counsellors is the Association for Student Counselling (ASC). Formed in 1970, the Association was established with the following aims:

1 to provide a professional organisation for anyone concerned with the counselling of students and young people;
2 to further the education and training of counsellors;
3 to further the study of counselling through research and the dissemination of knowledge;
4 to promote the acceptance of counselling in tertiary education;
5 to establish and maintain contact with other professional bodies in sympathy with the aims and objectives of the Association.

An elected executive committee carries out the major policy work of the Association, which is one of the divisions operating under the national 'umbrella' organisation of the British Association for Counselling (BAC). Sub-committees of ASC have the following responsibilities:

1 accreditation;
2 advisory group to institutions;
3 conference committee;
4 further education;
5 publicity;
6 research.

The Association is very active and provides a forum for discussion of a whole range of important issues. In addition to regular newsletters and conferences, the Association also publishes relevant papers and provides professional support for members.

OTHER 'SUPPORT' SYSTEMS FOR STUDENT COUNSELLORS

For many years the Association has encouraged the formation of regional networks, where student counsellors agree to meet, perhaps on a termly basis, to discuss matters of topical interest and concern. These support networks can be invaluable to those who attend in a variety of ways: from the sharing of information to being emotionally supportive; from sharing ideas of problem resolution to discussing issues of educational policy.

Finally and most recently (1990), the Heads of University Counselling Services have organised themselves, as a section of ASC, to meet to discuss matters of particular concern, especially those of management and policy. It is hoped that this small organisation will be able to stimulate discussion with employers and their professional bodies on pertinent issues.

DISCUSSION ISSUES

1   Explore the differences and similarities between the activities of tutoring and student counselling. What are the important aspects that distinguish these two educational activities?
2   What kinds of background and experience do you consider would be particularly useful for working in this setting?
3   What might be the benefits to the individual of joining a professional organisation of student counsellors?

Part II

STUDENTS AND THEIR
PRESENTING PROBLEMS

2

Transitions and Transformations

There is something exhilarating about working in higher and further education. One refreshing aspect is the regular influx of new and interesting clients who are intellectually gifted, often youthful in years, almost always so in spirit and who, generally speaking, are moving forward in a purposeful way towards goals, one of which will be an educational qualification. Although counsellors may see a small number of students for several years, we know that most of our clients will soon be moving on like the character in Milton's poem, Lycidas:

> At last he rose, and twitch'd his Mantle blew:
> To-morrow to fresh Woods, and Pastures new.

This chapter will consider the way in which the transient nature of student life and the particular developmental stages through which students will be progressing interact with each other to create a period of transformation. This transitional period in a person's life can be traumatic as well as exciting. An understanding of the background changes with which students are grappling helps counsellors to assess the impact and severity of presenting problems and the need for counselling. Similarly, the impact of academic demands and the academic calendar are other background factors which influence the progression of a student's problems as well as affecting the kind of counselling commitment a counsellor can realistically make. It is important to take a perspective on student difficulties informed by such environmental and developmental information because, otherwise, a novice counsellor may either overreact by prematurely referring to a psychiatrist a student who is temporarily (and perhaps, appropriately) distressed, or may wrongly attribute serious symptoms of profound malaise to exam stress or 'settling-in' problems. The role of this chapter, then, is to create a framework for the reader to picture the normal stresses and strains of student life so as to better appreciate the impact of specific problems which will be outlined in the next chapter.

CHANGE AS A STRESS FACTOR

Change of any kind is one of the most significant stress factors in life, and students are faced with a whole spectrum of transitions which they must negotiate. A useful way of understanding the concept of transition is to think of it as a period of moving from one state of mind where one feels secure about the knowledge and skills one possesses, through an interval of self-doubt and uncertainty, before confidence and understanding is regained. This involves temporary loss of a sense of personal effectiveness, and a stage of anxiety and confusion when old rules no longer prevail and previous ways of behaving seem to be less adequate, before new learning occurs and fresh possibilities appear on the horizon. The separation from family when a student moves away from home and the establishment of a new supportive network is the first, and often most important, transition which jumps to mind but there are many others.

DIFFERENT DEVELOPMENTAL STAGES THROUGH WHICH STUDENTS WILL BE PASSING

Who am I? Identity formation

We often think of life as consisting of stages. Each phase in life emphasises particular significant relationships or concepts which seem to be critical to the moment. The successful outcome of each phase paves the way for the next stage in life and the turning point or transition stage is a fragile time involving a push-pull dynamic between an earlier trend and the dawning of new, perhaps even opposing tendencies. The bulk of students in higher and further education fall within the 16–22 years age category which spans adolescence and the beginning of early adulthood. The tasks for mid to late adolescence include the formation of a sense of individual identity, acquired by struggling and experimenting with the question 'Who am I?' The crystallisation of a sense of self takes place in a context within which the peer-group exercises a strong influence on the individual and may demand conformity to a group identity. It is a time when a great deal of emphasis is placed on who is 'in' and who is 'out'. This is a burning issue for some first-year students, particularly those living in halls of residence, who may experience conflicts of allegiance to different friends or may even experience some mild but agonising form of social bullying. This occurs when there is a dominant social clique, for example, on one corridor in hall, which may become very close and cohesive but which appears exclusive and unfriendly to those who are not part of the set. The young person would be on target developmentally if able to emerge from this stage with an integrated image of him or herself as a unique person without recourse to over-identification with a sub-group. To achieve this maturity the personality develops through a process of unfolding which can at times seem more like a frantic to-ing and fro-ing between different beliefs, sets of friends, styles of dressing and contradictory conclusions about what is important and of value.

Students may feel the need to belong so markedly that they find themselves part of social groups whose values are really at odds with their own. They can become 'stuck' within such a group and appear to be identified with it in such a way that they then start to feel trapped and also rather lonely. Other students can adopt a superior and lofty attitude as a defence against their own feelings of inadequacy at being unable to find common ground and to make friends. It is important for counsellors not to collude with any statement which appears to confirm stereotyping of particular groups or to be misled by the image someone adopts and to allow the client freely to explore how they want to develop a sense of self and which bits of themselves they want to advertise publicly to the world. Involvement with religious societies, political organisations, animal welfare groups, not to mention identification with some music or fashion trends, is often, in part, related to the need to work out, on many different levels, the values and beliefs which will become a part of the sense of self.

Love, sex and friendship

Another phase of early adulthood poses the issue of loosening the close bonds with family and achieving a comfortable and appropriate level of intimacy with similar-aged peers. There are risks inherent in both too much detachment, leading to isolation and loneliness, and too much closeness, resulting in feelings of ensnarement in powerful relationships for which the individual may not be prepared. At this time partnerships, in terms of friends and sexual or romantic attachments, assume vital importance in the psychological foreground while in the background a tension may develop between the desire to co-operate and be the same as friends and the urge to compete and distinguish oneself from them and other peers. Successful transition through this stage allows the individual to form close and lasting relationships and eventually to make other commitments such as to a career or a consistent view of the world.

One of the main presenting problems in the counselling service where the authors work is that of relationship difficulties. Learning to make a commitment, however limited, to another person, is cause for great excitement, yet is also painful and upsetting. To deal with broken commitments and rejection or indeed to learn how to end relationships is traumatic at the best of times, but especially so when there are so many other issues with which to contend or if unresolved childhood experiences are obstructing the problem-solving process. Transformation into a sexually 'competent' being is also a matter of negotiating a transition which goes on well into adulthood. Young people often have unrealistic expectations of themselves, particularly within the domain of intimate relationships.

Continuity: time present and time past

As he or she matures, the young person revisits problem areas outstanding from much earlier stages, such as the striving for more independence from the mother or main carer of earlier childhood. There is established a sense of personal continuity or history, with a perspective of one's past, present and future unravelling sequentially. The outstanding and disruptive traumas of childhood are, ideally, put into perspective, and finally an adult sexual identity is founded as a basis for future, stable, intimate relationships. Counselling services are familiar with problems relating to all of these issues, especially to problems which have their roots in childhood traumas or current difficulty in relationships, both of which monopolise much of our attention. The reactivation of childhood dilemmas, especially where abuse has occurred, provides the student with an opportunity to work through disturbing emotions if they are able to make use of counselling or psychotherapy and can tolerate the increase in stress when they first become clients. It is very often only when a young person has left home that he or she can begin to come to terms with unhappy family situations, parental failures and relationship difficulties.

Leaving home

The bridge from childhood to adulthood needs to be robust enough to permit the young person to travel back and forth freely between family and the new life and between earlier stages and present ones. This means that families have to learn to let go of their children as well as young people being prepared for greater independence. Where the family has not been a secure place from which to launch oneself into the wider world because of family problems, relationship breakdowns, death or illness, the student may become stuck and confused. Sometimes when home life has been particularly unsupportive a student is bowled over by the discovery that getting to college is not the straightforward escape they planned, for they bring with them the unfinished business from their past. Just at a time when young people are leaving home there may be, occasionally, an unfortunate coincidence in that one parent suffers a major illness or dies. The effects of this are usually understood by friends and staff at the college or university. However, the loss of a parent and a fixed, permanent home-base from which to leave is also bewildering and painful when it occurs as the result of divorce or separation. Students often feel embarrassed to be upset by what parents have planned would be a civilised split 'when the children have left home' and struggle to know how to manage divided loyalties, their own dependency needs and the pressures from parents for support and understanding from their children.

THE ACADEMIC INSTITUTION'S IMPACT ON THE STUDENT

Learning to manage freedom

The bulk of full-time students in higher education will normally be engaged in the aforementioned profound personality developments while at the same time making all sorts of concrete and more evident adaptations. Such adjustments are very wide-ranging and encompass: leaving home; learning to cook and take care of themselves; finding ways to fit in or not with students with whom living arrangements are shared; discovering that there are many other, perhaps more gifted competitors; tasting the dangers and excitement of their own sexual, and to some extent, financial freedom; and finding how to work and take care of themselves without the support of structures imposed from above by teachers and parents. The changes in academic routines and teaching styles alone can precipitate anxiety in students who have been used to winning approval from closely involved teachers and gaining a sense of personal worth from high grades. Some students temporarily 'go to pieces' when faced with timetables which include only half a dozen lectures a week and struggle to find a method of disciplining themselves and directing their own study. Freedom can seem like a great burden and responsibility.

Coping with competition

Academic difficulty can cover a multitude of problems which may connect to a crisis in the search for a secure sense of identity when the clever student is faced for the first time with academic failure. Who is this person who thought of him or herself for so long as one who was good at his or her preferred subject and who may have clung onto this idea as one of the few certainties in life? The big fish in the little pool now has to swim with larger fish. Furthermore, individual achievement through competition and excellence is not a universally accepted concept and is seen differently in some cultures and some social classes. In the predominantly white, western

20

and middle-class milieu of a university there is a prevailing attitude which is ambivalent about success. The academic ideal is to be brilliant but without having to work too hard at it! However, the reality is that academic success is more likely to be related to perspiration and hard work than to inspiration or raw natural talent at all levels.

The role of the academic calendar

The developmental tasks outlined previously are augmented by the need to meet challenges presented by each stage of the academic course and the academic calendar. The difference in status from year to year is recognised in the American nomenclature used for each year of study with years one to four categorised respectively as freshmen, sophomores, juniors and seniors. Adjustments are needed to settle into the first year and then to adapt again to the demands of each ensuing year. A survey of UK first-year university students revealed that 60–70 per cent suffered from homesickness following their move to college. This topic is dealt with more extensively in Chapter 3, but suffice to say that this period can be an extremely difficult one for 'freshers'.

The second year, too, is famous for the 'second-year blues' when students become despondent with their courses or disillusioned with their friends. This is a time when the attractions of sharing a house or having contracted into a close and restrictive intimate relationship can begin to pale.

The final year brings a different set of tasks, requiring consistent focusing of effort and decision-making about the future. At the end of the course students make the transition to leaving student life, to seeking or beginning employment, and must learn to let go of what, in some respects, is a prolonged adolescence.

Counsellors might expect to see different problems at different stages of the academic course. Problems about course choice are commonplace in the first year but would be less usual and perhaps more alarming to counsellors if brought by a student in the final year.

Most people imagine the exam period to be a hectic time in counselling services. Indeed, it is a time when referrals need rapid attention and when crises abound but there are also, paradoxically, relatively quiet intervals between crises. There is often a break in the routine work to give students time to prepare for the exams and new clients rarely opt for starting counselling at this stage of the year. Moreover, students who are known to have difficulty with exams will, hopefully, have embarked upon counselling at an earlier date to give themselves an opportunity to prepare.

Institutional responses to student needs

The transformations affecting students are not simply one-way processes. Institutions themselves have to respond to the student population if they are able to provide education which is meaningful. Although learning is both an emotional and intellectual experience which has its roots in early infancy, educational establishments have a tendency to treat the emotions as a rather unfortunate accessory to otherwise effective intellects. Sometimes the content of some seminars and coursework is deeply upsetting to students who are expected to deal with issues such as violence to women and child abuse in abstract academic ways.

Moreover, we expect students to conform and play the academic game according to the established rules at just an age when they are floundering their way to becoming more distinct and more independent in outlook. At times it is difficult to distinguish healthy student rebelliousness from determined self-destructiveness on the part of students who resist conforming to academic criteria.

Moving on

Some of the most difficult transitional problems which student counsellors are consulted about are centred on issues to do with leaving the college prematurely and exiting from student life. All sorts of material may be hidden behind a student's usually sudden decision not to sit finals or to take part in a self-defeating way by merely writing their name at the top of the exam paper and then walking out. If the student has not actually appeared for finals it is sometimes possible, with the support of academic colleagues, to arrange for the student to defer, but if they have gone so far as to participate in the exams it is very hard to recoup anything. This can be one of the occasions when a counsellor really wishes she could turn back the clock and enable the student to rebel in a less destructive way at an earlier developmental stage.

One example of the way a student's dilemmas may be acted out is illustrated by the story of Dean, a young African-Caribbean man, about to sit his finals, who asked to see a counsellor. He had stopped attending lectures several months previously, had cut himself off from contact with family and friends and was about to make a decision to leave university without completing his degree. He talked about his childhood experiences of growing up in the only black family in his village and the racism that he met. He had become an activist in the black community in the city to which he had moved as an adult and thought that university would be useful to his aspirations both on a personal level and to further the cause of the people with whom he identified himself strongly. After three years his perspective had changed and he now felt himself to be declassed and marginalised within his community (he also felt very alienated from the university). It would be nice to describe how he was helped to resolve these serious issues and how he found a path out of what seemed to be a quagmire. In fact he refused to sit his exams and left the university without further explanation. The counsellor had to respect the decision he made. He did not want to become a client and so the meanings of what he was doing were not fully explored nor was it possible to help him find his own ways of integrating his newer sense of self with his past self.

TENSIONS BETWEEN DEVELOPMENTAL NEEDS AND ACADEMIC WORK

Assessment of the extent to which clients can cope with exploratory psychotherapy or the counselling process while pursuing an academic career is of great importance to student counsellors, who are likely to look for the most immediate and pressing issues on which to focus interventions rather than searching for underlying problems which require longer-term work. There is often a subtle shifting of focus between therapeutic needs and the demands of study or exams which is perhaps alien to counsellors who work outside of educational settings. Ellen Noonan (1986) talks of the 'dominance of the academic task in the strategy of the therapy and in the mind of the therapist' and explains that

> a fundamental task of the therapist in a university is to resist temptation to split the emotional and intellectual elements of the student, when it would be less stressful to do so and when the resistances to mending the split are strong and institutionalised.

This means that student counsellors are keen to promote a vision of the student as a whole person and to advocate counselling as a holistic process integral to education in the widest sense.

WOMEN STUDENTS: SAME OR DIFFERENT TRANSITIONS?

Some feminist therapists, particularly those based at the Stone Center in the United States, propose that a developmental pattern for late adolescence which fits for young women's psychological growth must take into account the psychological evidence which suggests that women develop on the basis of extending relationships rather than breaking away from them. Working from 'a self-in-relation model' (Jordan *et al.* 1991) women's core sense of self is seen as emerging out of a process of being in relationship. Although this 'interacting sense of self' is probably present in both sexes it may be discouraged in boys within western culture. The significance of this understanding is that women's sense of self is elaborated and refined not through a series of separations but through the inner experiences of relationships marked by a sense of connectedness to others. One implication is that daughters do not really need to be able to turn away from the mother–daughter bond as such but do need to transform it and to create other strong ties at the same time.

According to the 'self-in-relation' model a young woman entering college would be faced with the task of maintaining continuity of relationship with the family at home within a changed situation where there is much less day-to-day shared experience. At the same time, she would be trying to establish a network of friends and contacts to recreate in the new environment a sense of connectedness and mutuality. The stress is shifted onto the intricacies of setting up new connections while maintaining old relationships which may become fragile, and away from the established idea that, in order to develop, schisms and separations must occur. In practical terms this could mean that the student who tries to establish close ties to a tutor could be legitimately seeking connectedness rather than simply expressing a symptom of being overly dependent.

Young women who are homesick, missing their friends or sisters could feel undermined by any counsellor inference that they are unable to resolve their dependency needs or are immature. Indeed, many women from Asian families feel there is little possibility of a truly fulfilling life outside of the extended family network.

The role of competition in development is also of particular importance for young women. American adolescent girls with high academic grades were found to be more likely to demonstrate symptoms of depression than boys with similar grades or girls with lower grade averages. Pressure to compete and the woman's needs to be in relation to peers may exert opposing pulls. However, we should not forget that there are other explanations possible for young, high-achieving women to be depressed, which may be more to do with stress caused by society's sexual stereotyping and sexual harassment or discrimination.

This chapter has considered some of the stressful transitions which students have to deal with during their college life. As in any other setting, good counselling or psychotherapy means meeting each client without rigid preconceptions. We need to bear in mind all the preceding points about developmental stages and transitions but then find a way of half-forgetting them in order to be fully available to the client and the material that is being brought.

DISCUSSION ISSUES

1 How might becoming a trainee counsellor or student put you in touch with the issues of transition mentioned above?
2 How do you think the counsellor should have responded to Dean's departure from the university?

3   How might developmental stages differ for men and
    women who grow up in families which do not correspond
    to the western model of the nuclear family?

3

Main Presenting Problems

PROBLEMS ABOUT PROBLEMS

Trying to categorise the problems student clients bring to the counselling service is a little like using a kaleidoscope: if you shift position slightly the picture falls into a different pattern. Most services across the country collect statistics and other data from which they can detect trends in their work. Indeed, the Association of Student Counsellors has set up a research committee for which one important task is the collection of such data, thus attempting to analyse and understand underlying implications for student counselling across the country. However, there are often significant differences between counsellors in approaching the classification of problems. Some services collect information about presenting problems as they are understood by either counsellor or client at first meeting, while others focus on central problem areas as they become defined during the process of counselling. The two emphases are connected but different. The impact of self-rating as opposed to counsellor rating must also skew the comparison across services.

The use of problem category lists by either party also predetermines the options in how a problem might be defined. An example would perhaps clarify what might at first sight seem rather subtle and unimportant: Sonya was a mature student studying a science subject. She came to the counselling service in a crisis: first-year exams were imminent and she had become so anxious that she could not work. She knew from previous experience that she would 'freeze' in the examination room and fail to respond to the questions on the paper. In many ways classification of this presenting difficulty was easy because the service simply noted that she wanted help with exam nerves. However, over a long period of counselling of more than twenty sessions, the central issues emerged as somewhat more extensive and profound. Sonya, the child of brilliant and rather famous parents, had suffered a disturbing adolescence which disrupted her school work and had made her a disappointment (she believed) to her parents. Her earlier difficulties had been so marked that she had received psychiatric treatment. When pressurised by her own fears of failure, the reality of exams and a tense and stormy relationship with a partner, she was thrown into a mental state whereby she was very frightened but also very threatening to others. Sonya's way of coping with her feelings was to find a 'culprit' or opponent and to attack them, usually verbally, but occasionally physically. Sometimes Sonya's mental state was so precarious that she was afraid she would break down and become unable to take care of herself as had occurred in the past.

A counsellor using a category list which looked at central problems may have noted a long-standing problem in self-esteem or in dealing with aggression or, simply, of anxiety management. Another counsellor might have seen Sonya's problems through the framework of developmental stages and have seen her struggle for an academic career as related to unresolved issues from an earlier period in her life. Both of these approaches would be useful but they might be recorded very differently in statistics and might have resulted in quite diverse counsellor strategies.

An interesting feature of Sonya's case is the role academic difficulty played in encouraging her to attend the counselling service. Study and exam problems can be usefully understood as 'symptoms' requiring both practical help as well as exploration about what the difficulty means for that individual and especially why it has become so difficult to find a solution. Counsellors will vary in how they respond to such problems but they will agree that an academic difficulty is normally complex and may be connected to any of the other categories of problems, from bereavement to relationship problems. The following sections of this chapter will look at a range of common problems, grouped into five main categories.

RELATIONSHIP DIFFICULTIES

Student life is a great time for meeting new people and expanding horizons. This also means that relationships can alter very quickly or can become a refuge from the stress of dealing with so many challenges. It is not uncommon for an insecure first-year student to wrap him or herself up tightly in a cosy love affair which helps him or her deal with the pressures of socialising, studying and being away from home. By the final year this life-enhancing bond may have become like a noose around the neck of one of the two. A break-up may be painful both for the person who is rejected at this critical point but also for the person who has to take the initiative. This often leaves both parties with limited options in terms of a social life if they have shared all their friends or if they have lived together and worse still, if they are on the same course. Learning how to get into intimate relationships, but just as importantly, how to leave them, is a major concern which takes individuals and sometimes couples into counselling. Part of the counsellor's task is to help the client learn from their emotional experiences, just as he or she will be learning, albeit in a different manner, from academic experience.

Relationships with parents and other family members are also a common cause of distress. The variations on this theme are too numerous to outline but two particular aspects spring to mind which are especially troublesome. The first is the pain caused to a son or daughter by internalising the parental role too early in life. He or she may feel overwhelming responsibility for the well-being of a parental figure while suffering emotional neglect of their own needs. The following case study illustrates the point.

Tricia was a very able student who seemed on the surface to have made many friends and to have adapted well to student life. Unfortunately, after the first year away from home, she started to feel depressed and to withdraw from relationships. She had become aware of how different her own family life was from that of her flatmates and felt both very hurt by their insensitivity to her and very envious of the parental indulgence they all took for granted. She dreaded every holiday she spent at home. Over a period of counselling it emerged that Tricia felt very out of place with other students and felt the need to hide her family problems and the extent of her own sad feelings. Her mother, whom she believed to be mentally ill, was a very demanding woman who tyrannised the family on the grounds that she had mental health problems but would not seek professional help. Tricia had been trained as her mother's attendant while obviously being totally unequipped for this difficult task, and would feel both exasperated and guilty towards her mother. It was not until she left home that the effects of the family situation really began to emerge for Tricia. This is a regular feature of student counselling: the longed-for escape brings all sorts of difficulties to the surface which have been subsumed under the quest to get away to a new life. It is especially hard to move on from the family when family relationships have never been supportive and the child has felt responsible for the nurturing at home. The student counsellor will need to be able to help the client face up to the effects of emotional abuse or deprivation in the past and yet remain hopeful of making the present different and more satisfying.

The second aspect of family problems which can loom large is when parents try to interfere, perhaps with valid reasons in their own minds, with the transition of the young person to student life. Counsellors often receive phone calls from distressed parents who would like the counsellor to step into an actively parental role on their behalf. This might include efforts to get the counsellor involved in motivating the student to work harder or to look after him or her because friends are not immediately forthcoming. Ideally, parents should be encouraged to express anxieties without interfering with the student's right to struggle independently with problems. Counsellors have to defend confidentiality avidly but diplomatically. Young people need time to work through issues on their own before resolving to get external help and, furthermore, a person must feel free to choose counselling rather than have it thrust upon them. If there is time to talk on the phone the counsellor often discovers that the parent is in more need of support and reassurance in effecting the transition than the adult child.

Other relationship-related dilemmas include how to get on with friends in shared houses or hall. At first glance this may seem to be simply a matter of learning how to be more assertive or acquire more sophisticated personal skills. Where counselling services are able to offer group-work or where the students' union organises personal effectiveness courses, a lot can be gained from attendance at these, as well as individual counselling. However, not all difficulties related to this area are resolved by skills improvement. Sometimes the difficulty presented is just the top layer of a whole range of issues to do with forming close attachments or living with people. Furthermore, in all institutions counsellors will come across those students who cannot mix at all. Some students will respond to social skills training groups while others may need the slow and lengthy process of counselling to help them identify the source of difficulty and to begin to formulate some working remedies. The most difficult people to help are those who never appear in the counselling service but whose behaviour, be it aggressiveness, social isolation or depression, makes other people very anxious. These situations are frustrating for all concerned and counsellors must be clear about the parameters of counselling and the constraints of the counsellor's role without abandoning the concerned parties. Counsellors may need to tolerate being considered quite unhelpful by colleagues who expect them to perform the tasks of a social worker. The work student counsellors patiently but persistently carry out to maintain professional standards is an essential feature of counselling in this particular setting.

Finally, regardless of social expertise, some people are very unlucky when they start college and manage to miss out on activities or accommodation where they might meet friends. Loneliness, especially combined with all the stresses of transition, can be a crippling problem for students. To some extent, homesickness is often implicated in continuing loneliness and more will be said of this later. While it is well known that students enjoy a range of entertainments and social opportunities, it is less commonly understood that taking oneself off to an 'event' without a friend in tow demands flair and confidence. Students who may arrive late at college and miss out on induction events, students who for a variety of reasons do not drink, and who therefore miss out on communal activities organised around the bar, those who are living in digs away from other students and many others besides may fail to connect up with people they feel comfortable with and then find it harder to keep trying as term proceeds and clannish groups begin to form. Counsellors may have advice to offer departments and students' unions on how to cater for the needs of those who end up on the margins, by organising special meetings or social opportunities.

ACADEMIC DIFFICULTIES

As mentioned earlier, academic problems can indicate psychological distress and may be linked to a host of other issues, in particular to a changing sense of self. Most counsellors would want to know about the specific problems the student is experiencing and may offer appropriate ideas about strategies to adopt but they will also want to know why difficulties are happening at this point in time and how the family and the student view academic work in general. Although there are many ways in which the counsellor can offer practical help either on an individual level or by referral to study skills groups or resource material, the obstacle to grapple with is often emotional in nature. Students rarely suffer from a deficit of knowledge about how to help themselves but may lack understanding of what the resistance inside themselves to putting this knowledge into practice means. It is not unusual for a student to find him or herself adopting, for the first time, a rather rebellious stance towards parental expectations. If this can be identified and discussed, clients may well be able to move on to less self-defeating ways of expressing themselves.

There are four broad categories of academic difficulty, some of which appear, on the surface, to demand straightforward solutions, comprising advice and referral to other colleagues such as academic tutors or careers officers. However, counsellors need to listen to the presentation of these difficulties with 'the third ear' and determine what else might be wrapped up in these concerns.

Four principal areas of academic concern

1 Impaired performance: study skills, writing, presenting, reading, producing work.
2 Exam problems: revision, pre-exam anxiety, exam technique and coping with exam panic.

3 Loss of motivation: apathy, course dissatisfaction, transfer.
4 Failure and its aftermath: disciplinary procedures, appeals, leaving college.

The practical help which can be offered is extensive and includes reference to useful books, audio and videotapes, as well as brainstorming sessions on alternative approaches to work, or relaxation-training as an aid to study. The delivery of clear information about procedures to follow if the student wishes to transfer course or leave altogether is essential if this option becomes necessary. Where counsellors are expected to fulfil a welfare and advice function it is important to keep up to date with the plethora of benefit changes which issue forth frequently from central government. Different counsellors will feel comfortable with different aspects of the work and it can be enormously helpful to be able to involve tutors and administrators to provide some of the specialised functions. In recent years, at Sheffield University, we have been able to call on the help of an occupational psychologist to run groups and see individuals who want to improve their time-management skills and study skills. Low self-image and confidence seem to underlie all kinds of apparently personal, organisation problems. Although practical help with academic problems can be helpful, the opportunity to explore the background to difficulties may be sufficient, in itself, to shift the student through a crisis, as is demonstrated in the following example.

Paul, a final year student, was referred to the counselling service by his project tutor during the second term. Over the previous four months, Paul had become rather down-hearted and could not bring himself to complete his project, which counted significantly towards his degree. He was close to the deadline and knew that if he did not soon submit work, he would lose marks, fall behind in his preparation for the finals and jeopardise his hitherto excellent chances of achieving a good degree. Paul was normally very hardworking and down-to-earth and unaccustomed to talking about his feelings. In the seven counselling sessions which he attended he surprised both his counsellor and himself by plunging into some extremely sad aspects of his personal history which involved the deaths of his mother and father. Leaving university would mean a huge wrench for Paul because he had made himself a safe and secure home and, just as he was obliged to do when several years younger, he would have to move on to an uncertain future. The sessions involved very little discussion of the concrete tasks of the project other than checking that progress was being made. A few weeks after starting counselling, Paul announced 'I don't know what you're doing in these sessions and I don't understand why, but it's working. I'm feeling much better!' Paul remained sceptical about counselling while proceeding to improve in mood and academic performance. He couldn't bring himself to his last session but sent a card some weeks later thanking the counsellor and informing her that he had not only attained a good degree but had managed to find himself a promising job.

EMOTIONAL AND PSYCHOLOGICAL PROBLEMS

This is a wide category which may cover all kinds of difficulty: anxiety; depression; eating disorders; adjustment to loss and bereavement; self-image; self-defeating patterns of behaviour; obsessional thinking; and also fears and stresses caused by ill-health or disability. There are probably significant troubles which have been missed off the list simply because the rich constellation of problems brought to a counselling service are such that even experienced counsellors are often surprised by something 'new' in the way of a dilemma. As the counsellor works successfully with one person with for example a problem related to sexual abuse, so she or he find themselves to have become the focus of requests from that client's friends to work with them on the same issues. This is a curious phenomenon which can skew the counsellor's perception of 'common' problems!

Most psychological and emotional presenting problems in further and higher education settings are similar to those in other settings, but because of the preponderance of young people there may be biases to disorders such as eating problems or self-harm which tend to be more frequently found amongst this age group. Each counsellor will feel differently about where the outer reaches of their expertise lie and some prefer to refer clients who are struggling with serious mental health issues to statutory mental health services. However, the disruption caused by terms and vacations, in conjunction with long waiting lists for NHS treatment, often mean that 'referral' takes so long that the counsellor is already underway with counselling people with severe difficulties before an NHS appointment becomes available. Where a student's life or health may be at risk, as in anorexia nervosa, the counsellor needs to be able to liaise effectively with the student's General Practitioner. Where student health services exist, there can be very successful teamwork between counsellor and doctor. As pressure grows on counsellors to see more and more students it becomes increasingly necessary to refer on but increasingly difficult to do so.

There are many tapes and books on the market which offer a self-help approach to a wide range of problems as well as local and national self-help organisations. All of these resources can be invaluable but, at the end of the day, regardless of what else is 'on offer', clients continue to ask for individual, ongoing counselling.

PROBLEMS LINKED TO TRANSITIONS

One major difference student counsellors experience in their work, in comparison to counsellors in other settings, is in how homesickness is a frequent factor in a client's malaise. A major body of research on the topic of homesickness was carried out by Dr Shirley Fisher in recent years. It was found that about 60 per cent of students questioned reported that they had suffered from homesickness, regardless of gender or age. For a small number (5–10 per cent) homesickness was prolonged and distressing. There seems also to be an association between pining for home and lowered levels of health, concentration and efficiency. Homesickness is present in second, third and fourth-year students although the frequency is reduced to between 30 and 40 per cent.

New academic demands cause 70 per cent of students to feel anxious and intimidated by the standard of work required. The two factors of homesickness and study problems combine to make the student feel, at times, overwhelmed. When other, long-standing, issues emerge too, the student can easily become depressed and forlorn.

Student counsellors can help individuals to adjust to

transitions and give up the constant preoccupation with thinking about home which usually accompanies homesickness, replacing such thoughts with more positive plans and ideas for increasing involvement in the new environment. More importantly, homesickness, along with some ideas about antidotes and prevention, can be highlighted as a 'normal' phenomenon in induction days. In this way, other staff can begin to develop useful ways of anticipating and reducing the potential for homesickness. More will be said about this in Chapter 7.

Another issue, related to transitions in terms of developmental stages, is the formation of sexual identity. The emergence of conflict or distress over both sexuality and sexual orientation is a regular problem brought to student counselling services. Moving away from home can furnish a student with the first opportunity to question the values and beliefs of their parents and friends. This means that a freedom is possible which can feel very threatening. The exaggeratedly promiscuous student, of either gender, the 'gender-bending' rebel, the middle-of-the-road person with a steady partner and the earnest scholar who seems to live mainly for work may all be struggling with fears about who they are sexually. Students often test out counsellors in subtle ways before plunging into the topic of sexual identity or, indeed, sexual practice. It is so common for clients to have doubts about this area as to appear quite 'normal'. Late adolescence can be a time to revisit old unfinished psychological business. The question 'Can I love someone of the same gender as myself or not?' and if so 'How do I meet other people like me?' needs to be approached with great sensitivity. The frequently encountered concern about whether or not a person is essentially gay or lesbian can be an introduction to many related but different worries. Some clients, experience tremendous guilt over their sexual feelings, regardless of sexual orientation or even of practice. The role of religion and cultural beliefs is closely involved in these matters. A number of students experience severe difficulty in resolving the issue of whether or not they should have sex before marriage. Counsellors need to feel quite relaxed about their own sexuality and sexual identity and their own personal code of conduct in order to be able to be receptive to clients who may want to talk about behaviour which is outside of the counsellor's own experience.

Sometimes clients want to talk very explicitly about sexual technique and again, it is not possible to be an expert on every aspect of sex therapy. Some of the current manuals and videos are informative and extremely detailed and a small collection of these could be a useful resource for a counselling service. However, most clients want to talk about their underlying feelings in regard to sex and how they think of themselves, rather than be given a course of instruction in 'how to do it'. A lot of people believe they ought to be highly skilled in the sexual arts despite their inexperience and can be self-critical when they fail to achieve sexual satisfaction. Finally, it is sometimes in connection to sexual problems that memories begin to emerge of childhood sexual abuse which has long since been repressed and which returns to consciousness in disturbing 'flashbacks'.

CRISES

Counselling services in higher education cannot truly fulfil a crisis intervention function because they are, generally speaking, too scantily resourced, and are staffed by counsellors who are trained in counselling and psychotherapy rather than crisis intervention. Nevertheless, in their own way, most counselling services try to meet the needs of clients who attend in a desperate hurry for help. Factors which precipitate a crisis are varied and include traumas such as rape and sexual assault, sudden bereavement, suicidal thinking and feeling, psychiatric emergencies and extreme reactions to examination stress.

Counselling services are often suggested to students in distress as one of the ports of call in an emergency. This can be an awkward occurrence as most counsellors work only during office hours and are dominated by a tight schedule of 'on-the-hour' appointments. Sometimes formal counselling is not the best option in a crisis when the wounded party needs love and reassurance from friends and relatives. In this respect, it is wise to take an 'ecological' view of counselling; that is, to foster the natural, supportive friendship and family networks around a person before promoting the more narrow, professional option of counselling. Whilst wishing to make themselves valued and respected, counsellors also need to avoid 'professionalising' personal pain and depriving other people of the opportunity to respond, or indeed, of enabling the 'victim' to find their own unique ways of coping.

There are no rules about how counsellors can best manage 'crises' except to plan for them by making sure there are spaces in the diary or the working day when no clients are booked in and the counsellor is free to see someone who is genuinely desperate. Safeguarding such times from clients and staff who are simply in a bit of a rush to be seen is quite an art for counsellors and receptionists! Good relationships with local GPs or student health services are essential for help, when necessary, in these cases. In fact, counsellors' ability to make good relationships with all manner of helping agencies is highly valuable.

More challenging is the necessity for the counsellor and the client to confront the limits of the counselling process. Although it is almost always useful to talk about painful experiences, it is not necessarily appropriate to do so immediately after a traumatic event. For example, a victim of rape may have undergone the ordeal of describing her experience several times to police officers, a doctor, friends and a tutor before being referred to a counsellor. The woman may prefer to withdraw a little into herself before choosing to speak to a counsellor. Sometimes, there is an expectation that the counsellor will be able to take away bad experiences or 'make it better' or indeed, the counsellor may be brought in because someone other than the client is unable to cope either with what has happened or with being powerless in the face of what has happened.

Where psychiatric crises are concerned, the counsellor may well need to involve others in the care of the client but will probably also want to stay involved for a little while, if not for a long time. Again, the counsellor's ability to form co-operative links with local services is helpful, although increasingly difficult to maintain as all agencies are overpressurised by demand. Often a very distressed person is much more able to cope with life after spending some time with a counsellor, talking through what is happening, or will then be more able to choose to seek out or accept other professional help. However, additional time is always needed for follow-up later. Building 'slack' into a diary is essential to permit both attention to crises and a minimal amount of follow-up.

THE REFERRAL PROCESS

The perusal of the problem categories listed above suggests, we hope, that most counsellors in further and higher education see their remit as being available to students and staff to carry out personal counselling at the request of the person with the problem. However, there are times when students do not want counselling and are 'sent' by a tutor. This difficult situation is discussed in Chapter 6.

Where a counsellor has a dual role as a teacher as well, there are even greater needs to protect the counselling service from intrusion by the demands of disciplinary processes or over-zealous tutoring. Under no circumstances should a student be forced into counselling. The Association for Student Counselling has produced a thoroughly useful handbook for managers who want to understand better how to evaluate their own counselling services and to appreciate the kind of situations where counselling cannot be delivered, even when it is desirable.

One function of a counselling service is to represent the 'caring' aspect of an institution. So long as staff feel there is an agency to which they can refer in times of crisis, problems seem more manageable and there is less stress. In reality, this agency may never be used by the student or the lecturer who has it in the back of his or her mind as a possible resource. There are other times, of course, when counselling is used and plays an important role in crisis defusion or prevention. It is likely that readily available counselling with only a short waiting period helps prevent problem situations from escalating.

As can be seen from the discussion above, the counsellor in higher and further education is not only concerned with a wide range of presenting problems but is also implicitly and explicitly involved with the process of education itself. Counsellors may feel strongly about their theoretical orientation and may practice in a 'purist' way but they will also be familiar with alternative methods of tackling problems and be able to provide such opportunities themselves or be able to refer on, if this is appropriate.

DISCUSSION ISSUES

1 How do you think the work of a student counsellor in higher education might differ from that of a counsellor working in a college of further education?

2 How would you respond to a student who came to ask you if you could motivate him or her to work?

3 What do you think might be the difficulties in setting up an exam skills workshop in a university?

4

Special Problems of Mature Students

INTRODUCTION

Some colleges of further and higher education and some of the new universities (former polytechnics) are justifiably proud of their record of widening access to groups of students traditionally underrepresented. The older universities are now competing on the same terrain and many students are now older in age and often described as 'mature' students.

The term 'mature' is misleading because it unfairly connotes immaturity in younger students and infers that older students have acquired some ephemeral quality which they themselves often feel is lacking. Whatever the age of the older student, she or he will feel at times inadequate, childlike and deskilled, and at other times, older and more experienced than fellow, younger scholars, sometimes fluctuating between these extremes within the duration of one seminar! The main background problems which influence mature students are financial hardship, relationship and family difficulties and the changing nature of how the student conceives of him or herself. Unfortunately, it is also not simple to clarify the age at which students are considered by institutions as mature. The ages 21, 23 and 25 all appear in different sets of regulations, thus adding further confusion for this group.

FINANCIAL DIFFICULTIES

It is a sad but true fact that some mature students are much worse off financially at university or college than in the dole queue or on income support. The financial costs incurred are terrifically high for those who have given up employment and for those whose financial status will suffer if they have been receiving unemployment and some other benefits to which they cease to be entitled upon entering higher education. In addition, taking three or four years out of employment can have consequences at a later stage when the student competes with much younger candidates for work and is handicapped in the eyes of some employers by age barriers. Many mature students are fully aware of the drawbacks and disadvantages to surmount in becoming a mature student and remain powerfully motivated to proceed despite the obstacles. Others comprehend only gradually the full financial and emotional implications, sometimes because of changes in legislation (of which there have been numerous in the last few years), one of the most detrimental being the withdrawal of housing benefit to students. Mature students need to be astute money-managers and to contend with the restrictions of the student budget and the accumulating debt of a student loan. When an unplanned expense is incurred, the student can find him or herself in a very precarious financial state. Where the student is responsible for dependents, who may be children, partners or elderly relatives, there can be stress and uncertainty spread through the whole family.

FAMILIES AND OTHER RELATIONSHIPS

Financial strain can exacerbate other background complications, especially where relationships and families are concerned. Part of the prelude to registering at university will be a complex unravelling and clarification of personal and career development needs. Sometimes the impact of being a student is a powerful blow to an already unsatisfactory marriage or family life. The network of relationships around a student, even where they have been supportive, has to be able to alter and adapt to the demands of the educational institute and to what is often the beginnings of a new personality emerging from the old, familiar one. Personal development can clash with the needs of other family members or partners who may not have chosen this particular opportunity for change and who may resent it being thrust upon them.

If late adolescence was not a spontaneous and exciting period the first time round it can be revisited with gusto at university. Mature students are just as likely as younger students to fall in love or become entangled in complex relationships. Indeed, there is some evidence which suggests that mature women students are more likely than younger women to become involved in a sexual liaison with teaching staff. Although both parties may be similar in age, there remains in such relationships a tremendous power imbalance. Students may believe they can manage the relationship because they are sophisticated and experienced. However, at the end of the day, if a lover has to mark work and allocate grades, the chances of a fair deal for all concerned are remote. Students frequently discover that the greatly admired member of staff establishes a fresh liaison in each new intake of students.

Resentment can be created amongst fellow students not only by romantic links between mature students and staff but also by friendships. Mature students are often confident in establishing socially comfortable relationships with teaching staff and may dominate classes to the detriment of others. On the other hand, some tutors may be younger, inexperienced and intimidated by older students. Alternatively, the mature student might feel such envy and jealousy about other younger students or about members of staff that they are unable to make the best use of seminars and tutorials. All of these potential relationship difficulties can mar the ability of the student to learn.

CHANGES IN SELF-PERCEPTION

Finally, the altered self-perception is an important fact to take into consideration with older students. Of course, this is usually seen as simply a positive development but during the course of studies, self-concepts will undergo so many fluctuations that the individual can feel hollow and out of touch with a consistent, inner sense of self. In order to learn, the individual must be able to tolerate not knowing or understanding, must be able to make mistakes and be prepared to fail. When someone is feeling deskilled or pressured by all sorts of constraints it is hard to manage this 'negative capability'. We can all have difficulty in this area, but mature students may have so much emotional investment in education and so many other burdens to shoulder that they can find their openness to new knowledge and learning severely restricted.

In a different vein, mature students may begin to blossom academically and emotionally and find that they have outstripped the people to whom they have felt close and may become estranged from them or rejected by them. A failing marriage may fall to pieces when one partner goes into full-time education. Making new close ties may feel as if it demands a lot of precious effort if the student is older and unused to being a 'singleton'. Some people refuse to use the students' union facilities because they cannot tolerate feeling unique in terms of age and dress!

The background factors surveyed have a tendency to interact with each other in an alarming fashion and are often implicated in the three principal concerns which bring mature students to the attention of counsellors. The first is the student response to the transition to university and the ensuing problem of adjustment. The second is academic difficulty. Finally, older students commonly present with relationship difficulties.

ADJUSTMENT TO A NEW ENVIRONMENT AND STUDENT ROLE

The first few weeks of the first term at college can be both exciting and disorientating. Students become mentally overwhelmed by a plethora of information, are daunted by large lecture theatres and dismayed by the crowds of undergraduates, the length of reading lists and the apparent lack of structure and direction in their timetables. Or, conversely, if they are in applied science faculties, they may baulk at the rigidity of their highly structured timetables.

Some people will be lucky enough to encounter friendly faces on the first day but may not see them again for weeks! At first sight, it may seem as if the student is the only representative of the over-21s on the premises. The overall effect is often that the student feels old, isolated, unsure about their motivation in registering and cannot concentrate properly on anything anyone tells them. This sense of becoming deskilled and incompetent, even at the simple task of finding a way around the institution, is also sometimes allied to minor physical ailments, tiredness and loss of vitality. These symptoms are all synonymous with the phenomenon of culture shock, like that experienced by international students, and eventually will subside with time.

In the early stages of a student's transition to academic life, counselling may be sought out in response to transitional problems which, if there is a history of emotional or psychological breakdown, can be misinterpreted as the harbinger of much more serious and long-lasting disruption. Contextualising this stressful period as being related to a kind of culture shock, and to the transitions described in Chapter 2, can help clients begin to understand and overcome temporary set-backs. Furthermore, forbearance of the vexations of this period can help the client to avoid hasty decision-making about leaving college or changing course. Similarly, if the transitions can be understood, the client is then more likely to be able to learn about themselves from this experience and bring that insight to bear on future transitional periods.

An important role for the counsellor is to make sure that orientation workshops are established both to welcome in new mature students and to give them opportunity to encounter other mature students and to think about how they will meet the challenges of becoming a student. As well as formal talks from the administration and student services, such orientation sessions can be an excellent time to get to know a few people and to pool fears and worries and potential solutions about diverse aspects of academic life. Counsellors are usually most adroit at conducting such sessions and facilitating 'ice-breaker' exercises, which, if left to inexperienced administrators to activate may rapidly become 'ice-makers'! These workshops can also introduce students to a planned timetable of future study skills or exam skills workshops, or social meetings or support groups, all of which will help new students feel integrated and welcomed into the institution.

ACADEMIC PROBLEMS

It is usually after a period of intense re-evaluation that a mature student undertakes to enter full-time study. The costs, emotionally and economically, of a degree course are such that a student will not tolerate readily a sense that she or he is falling behind with academic work. Failure can be sharply experienced for several reasons: (1) the disappointment invoked in recognising that undertaking the course is an altogether different experience to the expectations that were harboured originally; (2) the effects of culture shock in the first year; (3) the likelihood of having experienced some degree of 'school failure' in the past, the feelings about which can suddenly be reactivated in the present; (4) difficulty in accepting criticism and feeling the need for more personal encouragement and validation than is routinely available in higher education; and (5) envy or misunderstanding from family and established friends who are unable to progress and adapt to the changing needs of the student and may want to undermine him or her.

This makes a difficult job for academic staff who have to be reassuring where appropriate but also be firm and clear about demanding good academic standards. Sometimes older students have arrived on courses after a great deal of personal interaction and encouragement from access tutors and others. It is necessary for them to learn to study in a more impersonal environment and to come to terms with the limits which exist on tutors' availability.

One particular problem which affects older students is the difficulty in keeping a perspective on the field of knowledge or study that has to be entered for any one piece of work. Trying to read, write or do too much in an academic sense is a temptation for someone who may be passionately interested in their subject. Learning to set realistic study goals and formulating clear guidelines about what is required in a piece of work is essential. Some older students are open about their difficulties and may well confront tutors about academic problems which other, more timid, students are also experiencing. The counsellor may need to help other students seek and accept help from tutors as well as assist staff in recognising the need to take a flexible approach to students.

Finally, part-time students can experience particular stress when their circumstances at work change (i.e., they might be promoted or change jobs) with the result that the commitment to academic work and the necessary time allocation required then becomes impossible to sustain.

RELATIONSHIP PROBLEMS

It is wonderful to see mature students, especially women who have been committed mainly to other people's development, begin to grow in confidence. Unfortunately, previous relationships can start to feel like a brake on the individual's self-actualisation. Partners may resent not only the time spent in study but moreover, the excitement and enthusiasm directed away from the home and the relationship. Children can miss the attention and care lavished on them in the past. Older dependents can, and frequently do, fall ill or die. Balancing the need to work, make new friends and socialise as well as to maintain established relationships and routines is precarious. The answer is often to lower standards and to prioritise commitments. Regularly, the 'common sense' approach to relieving stresses at home has already been attempted and the client is faced with the issue of whether or not to leave a relationship or whether or not to leave college.

Relationships with the family of origin can become strained as the mature student takes a critical perspective on attitudes and behaviours which were once taken for granted. The dawning realisation that perhaps the individual has been held back or even exploited by family attitudes can produce rifts in the family and leave the individual feeling angry and rejecting. Social science undergraduates who are mature often respond to psychological and sociological projects in an intensely personal way and use some of the academic ideas to help them think through their own development and past history.

Even where academic work is satisfactory, some mature students seem to be disposed to have personality clashes with others. Those who have been accustomed to directing others prior to becoming students may find it hard to institute more informal working relationships and can become isolated and lonely. Social events organised by groups such as Mature Students' Associations can be a solution but will obviously not appeal to everyone. There are surely many other kinds of relationship problems which mature students struggle with but perhaps these will suffice to give the reader a brief picture of the dilemmas involved. A short case study may bring some of the issues to life.

Bernadette was 33 years old. She had left school at 16 with several 'O' levels to her name and had then worked as a secretary. She had realised over the years that she would always be bored in the jobs that she did and had studied at night school to gain good 'A' levels. She bought a small house located very near the university department with which she had registered. Although apparently a sociable and out-going young woman, she had always suffered from low self-esteem and a poor self-image and believed herself to be exceptionally unattractive to the opposite sex. She was highly self-critical and deprecating about her abilities and her looks. Bernadette missed out the 'freshers' week and induction programmes because she wanted to work right up to the last moment so that she would be more at ease financially.

University was a great shock to Bernadette who felt bewildered and overawed by the large numbers of undergraduates in her lectures. She thought everyone was viewing her from the same disparaging perspective that she took about herself. Since her house was so close by she would often skip lectures and retreat home. She considered the students' union to be virtually out of bounds to her since it was thronged by hundreds of seemingly 'young, gifted and beautiful' 18-year-old students. A pattern began to develop: she avoided more and more lectures, never attended tutorials, where she felt she would be even more conspicuous, and would have panic attacks if she tried to force herself to go into the largest of the lecture theatres. When Bernadette attended the counselling service she had missed most of her first year's work, knew no other students from whom to borrow notes and was on the verge of giving up university altogether. She was reluctant to approach academic staff who she thought would consider her to be a time-waster because she had missed so many lectures and seminars. Clearly, there were some underlying features in Bernadette's case which were unrelated to her status as mature student and which caused her much anguish, but other factors such as her social isolation and the effect of those first few weeks of not settling in at college were particularly related to her being a mature student.

Counselling involved helping Bernadette to investigate the negative way in which she viewed herself while, at the same time, encouraging her to construct strategies to deal with the incipient crisis of first-year exams, for which she was totally unprepared. Fears about how other people might see her were explored and ideas tested out in reality. A group project which she had been avoiding was entered into and much to her surprise, Bernadette began to make friends on her course. Too much academic work had been missed so she opted, with the endorsement of the counselling service, to resit her first year. The combined effect of making friends and being supported in thinking about and taking action over issues she had been responding to by means of avoidance behaviour allowed Bernadette to successfully, and by all accounts, happily, retake her first year.

MATURE STUDENTS – PROBLEMS FOR THE COUNSELLOR?

Mature students attend counselling services for help with a variety of difficulties, some of which may have been troubling them for years. When they discover that counselling can be useful they may then exert a lot of pressure on the counsellor to provide long-term therapy. Sometimes such an arrangement is desirable, but given the scant resources of counselling services in education, the offer of a lengthy period of counselling needs to be weighed carefully against the pressure of waiting lists and the necessity to maintain modest, serviceable goals. Mature students often reside locally or adopt the college or university town as their new home. This means that they can attend for counselling during vacation periods. These two factors may render counselling of mature students much more akin to counselling in private practice (except, of course, the student does not make the sacrifice of paying directly for this service). The counselling relationship may thus become a very powerful one.

Even in shorter-term work with mature students, there may be attempts to get the counsellor to collude with the client about the irresponsibility and immaturity of younger students or the unreasonableness of tutors. Trying to make a friend of the counsellor is another seductive ploy older students may use to avoid really facing up to the need to change something about themselves. Some mature students may feel as envious of the counsellor as they do about lecturers, which can hold them fast in a rut both emotionally and academically. All of these points are equally true for younger people but seem more preponderant amongst older clients.

Occasionally, mature students, perhaps a little more frequently than their more youthful peers, try to play the educational system in order to swing some kind of benefit. It is always hard to determine what is being sought when someone books in to see a counsellor and after the first session requests a letter to a faculty requesting special treatment because they are 'in counselling'. Each case should be taken on merit but as a rough guide, a request for a letter after one interview often evokes scepticism.

There are, fortunately, many instances when counselling mature students is not only rewarding but plainly effective. To witness the progression through periods of enormous self-doubt and temptations to withdraw from education to self-confidence and achievement of goals is a delight. Mature students do seem to find it possible to benefit from the educational experience in a holistic way.

DISCUSSION ISSUES

1 What do you imagine might be some of the feelings invoked in a mature student client by finding the counsellor to be much younger than him or herself?

2 How would you respond to a mature student's request to be seen in your lunch hour because she cannot find any other space in your diary which suits her and fits in with her child-care arrangements?

3 A mature student tells you, during the counselling session, that she is having an exciting love affair with her head of department, and is thinking of revealing this to her husband as a preliminary to moving in with her lover. What are your first thoughts and what do you say?

5

Special Problems of International Students

INTRODUCTION

Imagine that you have just gained a scholarship to pursue your studies in your favourite subject at an overseas university. You are delighted. Your family and friends are excited also and very supportive of the idea. The scholarship seems most generous in financial terms and it looks as if some money will be left over, after tuition and living expenses are accounted for, to enable you to travel whilst in that country.

The information you have already received from the university is well presented and attractively published. Visually stunning photographs of the campus are accompanied by exciting accounts of activities that you can become engaged in whilst studying there.

All is set for a wonderful three years.

Amidst great excitement and some tears of apprehension and sadness that you will miss your loved ones, you finally embark on your flight to this great adventure.

The experience of departure leaves you in a somewhat reflective and contemplative mood which predominates most of the flight. The captain announces that arrival is imminent, requests the fastening of seat belts and surveys the weather conditions in London. It is raining, cold and grey!

A slight hassle, going through immigration control, as they check and question your papers and then you are confronted by . . . nothing that is familiar. The advertisement hoardings are not in your language, people are dressed differently, the signs are somehow different to your own country and in addition to all this, you have got to find your own way, via

51

underground and surface trains to your new college, some two hundred miles distant.

We ask you, the reader, to try to imagine yourself in the student's shoes as they have to tackle situation after situation (seeking directions, buying tickets, finding trains) in a different language and on their own.

Fortunately the journey is managed without too much difficulty and you are met, at the station, by large banners welcoming new students to the college. Now pretty tired, having been travelling for fourteen hours, you are relieved that your college is one of those that has extended their welcome to such reception arrangements.

A minibus ride, forms to sign in the college housing office, another ride and at long last you reach the room which is to be your home for the forthcoming year. Like London, Heathrow, it is still grey outside and unfortunately grey inside! When you have a moment you will put posters on the wall, to make it more homely, you think to yourself. These are your last thoughts as you crash into sleep, exhausted and with very mixed emotions. You are now on your own. You cannot go home for at least a year. You have no friends in this country. You have a different skin colour. You have a different language. Your culture is different. Everything in life is now going to be different, twenty-four hours a day, to what you have ever experienced before.

It is no wonder that international students consult student counsellors during their stay in the UK. Indeed it is incredible that their drop-out rate is not a lot higher, given the considerable personal, cultural and academic challenges they will have to face to succeed in their aims.

CULTURE SHOCK

Already, from the above introduction, we can begin to see that the process of settling to study in a new country might be anything but smooth!

Culture shock has become a much-used phrase in recent years. In simple terms it describes the impact upon a person of a new culture. The psychological and emotional phenomena that accompany culture shock can be likened to the effects of other transitional phases in life. A classic example is that of homesickness, already referred to in Chapter 3. The cumulative effects of change in life are stress-producing.

So how might culture shock affect the international student that we have described above? Parallel to other psychological models of transition (bereavement, loss of employment, loss of limbs, etc.) the stages through which we go as human beings, though describable, are not fully predictable in their sequence or duration, making this process an uncomfortable experience for clients and perhaps a confusing one to their immediate friends and family.

Initially, our student may enjoy a 'honeymoon' period in which their new experiences are exciting and wonderful. Certainly, many institutions organise various welcoming receptions and special social events which would key into a honeymoon period. During the first few days and sometimes weeks there will be lots to do and people to meet.

International students might enjoy the honeymoon period for quite some time. However, during this first stage they will begin to have a range of experiences with other people, staff and students at the college, that leave them a little confused and not understanding. They might find that the differences in communication become impactful and cannot be screened out. Confusion, disorientation, loss, apathy and a sense of isolation are the emotional states that accompany this transition into the second stage, 'disintegration'. The student may experience tremendous temptations to withdraw and may become depressed.

Research carried out some years ago by the United Kingdom Council for Overseas Students Affairs indicated that international students consult their doctors very frequently during their first year of study here. This factor is clearly a manifestation of culture shock in action.

The third stage is named 'reintegration'. This is a crucial developmental stage as it involves the person affected in a consolidation of their own self. They reject the differences they are experiencing, and can begin to feel anger, rage, nervousness and accompanying anxiety. Their behaviour can thus become hostile, rejecting, suspicious and rebellious. Despite the negative-sounding nature of these characteristics, this process enables the person to reaffirm themselves and their own identity. It is a stage where the energy of anger is expressed outwardly rather than consumed internally.

Student counsellors, inevitably, will be approached by international students in the grip of the culture shock process. They may be depressed or angry and have many other emotions in between. Additionally, the concerns they bring might span a vast range of subjects and may include implicit and explicit criticisms of the host culture. Student counsellors can find themselves in a difficult position, personally and therapeutically.

How do they feel about having their culture attacked? Can they identify with the student's perspective that the food is awful and that the water is not suitable for drinking? What reactions might the counsellor have to being told that all staff in the college are not polite, certainly not friendly and indeed some are quite dismissive of international students?

A knowledge of the culture shock model can help the counsellor understand the general psychological and emotional upheaval that can affect international students. However the counsellor has to decide how best they might respond to the student and if it would be of value to share the model with them. This provision of information can be most helpful to the suffering person. It might help to explain their present emotional experience of life. However, delivered at the wrong time, the client may feel that the counsellor is not comprehending their predicament, is not understanding their view of things and is certainly not responding to the actual problems they have brought to counselling. All they are doing, the student might feel, is responding with inappropriate information that does not change the situation they are in!

The final stages of culture shock, 'autonomy' and 'independence' are less dominated by negative emotions and represent psychological and emotional development towards the legitimation and valuing of cultural difference. Self-assurance, a renewed sense of independence and a capacity to become expressive and creative typify these fourth and fifth stages. In the fifth stage the person has achieved what is called 'bicultural competence', a capacity to feel competent and at home in both cultures. This is a very sophisticated stage to achieve and there is no guarantee that everyone will reach it, as the following story indicates.

One of the authors was consulted by a mature student who had been seconded by her employer to undertake a Masters degree. She had been resident in Britain for eighteen years, having migrated during her late teens. During one of the counselling sessions she had referred to long periods of depression after arriving in the United Kingdom which had lasted for many years. Bearing in mind that this episode had been referred to before but never dwelt on in the counselling, the counsellor decided to tell her about the above model of culture shock. The response couldn't have been more encouraging!

'Why didn't they tell us?', she exclaimed, 'I have been here eighteen years. For the first twelve years I was seriously depressed, I had a complete range of anti-depressant drugs, I was hospitalised for a while, I was given electro-convulsive therapy. That is the first explanation I have come across that makes sense of my experience. Even now I think that I am only in the fourth stage . . .'.

THE EFFECTS OF CULTURE

According to Raymond Williams in his book *Keywords*, culture is 'one of the two or three most complicated words in the English language'. This is so because of a range of factors, from the historical origins of the word to the many developments it has undergone in different disciplines.

There were over 150 definitions of the word 'culture' in the social sciences by the 1960s. A brief but succinct definition has been developed by Hofstede that defines culture as the 'collective mental programming of a people'.

Culture profoundly affects all aspects of behaviour, shapes beliefs, forms expectations and locates perception in specific ways. When two culturally different people meet many complications can arise between them. We behave in certain ways, we believe certain things, we know what is and what is not polite. What we don't appreciate, at a conscious level, is not only that our patterns of behaviour are strongly culturally determined, but that they can differ markedly and subtly from other cultures' perspectives.

A dramatic example of this difference was experienced some years ago by a student counsellor who was being consulted by an African student. Having seen the counsellor for several sessions before the summer vacation the student announced that upon his return home he would consult a witch-doctor. The initial impact of the term 'witch-doctor' upon the counsellor was quite dramatic.

Indeed it was tempting to her to immediately discourage the student from going. Upon reflection, however, she was influenced by her own deep belief in the inner wisdom of individuals (that people can be trusted to find the help they need) and in her own knowledge and experience of therapeutic forms not traditional to British culture (e.g. shiatsu and acupuncture).

Major examples of cultural differences include patterns of non-verbal behaviour (greetings, patterns of eye contact, gestures), interpersonal space, the different perceptions of time and the effect of the context in which people meet. Culture also affects our capacity to deal with people in authority, to be comfortable with gender role differences, to tolerate uncertainty and to be members of a group. There are many other differences between cultures and any one can prove a barrier to intercultural understanding and communication.

THE CULTURE OF STUDY

Based upon the above it should be no surprise to appreciate that international students can experience considerable difficulty in coming to terms with the dominant patterns of further and higher education in the United Kingdom, as these very systems are also determined by the dominant culture. Much of the educational activity that students are involved in demands that they work on their own, and as such, academic work becomes competitive. These dimensions, in part, reflect the fact that Britain is a highly individualistic country; students are expected to demonstrate self-sufficiency, independence of thought and a capacity to articulate and defend their views on a range of subjects.

International students who have been educated at school in their home systems will have had a very different range of experiences which will have shaped their expectations of what education is and how learning is assessed.

A West African student consulted a student counsellor in a considerable state of anxiety. He had written what he considered an excellent piece of work. However, the lecturer had given the essay a borderline pass. The student could not understand this wide difference in appreciation of the essay. Invited by the counsellor to talk about essay-writing in his own country he explained that intelligence was demonstrated by writing 'laterally', that is, by following different trails of thought in different directions. The wider the range of data that could be included, the better. The contents of an essay, therefore, spread outwards from the title. Once this was explained, the counsellor was able to see that the student was operating upon a culturally different system of essay composition than that prevalent in the United Kingdom.

Counsellors may often hear complaints from tutors that they feel that international students require 'spoon-feeding'. Behind these assertions often lie resentment and non-understanding. Many tutorial staff will not have considered the fact that their teaching and their expectations of students are culturally determined and indeed have been reinforced by years of teaching. Counsellors can not only help individuals and groups of students with these factors but they are in a position to offer insights to staff gained from their experience of work with international students. Examples of such work with staff are given in Chapter 6.

LANGUAGE AND UNDERSTANDING

Alongside the impact of moving to another country and the effects of cultural difference sits the most significant challenge that most international students have to face: that of language. Some international students, do, of course, come from English-speaking countries and seemingly experience an easier transition process. Unfortunately, however, their specific linguistic difficulties are not likely to be appreciated by UK staff and students. As one American student said recently to one of the authors, 'I thought I would face no problems with understanding, as I speak English. However, what with accents, local sayings and this regional accent, I am really lost. Teachers even talk about rubbers in the lecture room (rubbers are condoms in the USA) and students sometimes ask if I have any fags (fag is an abusive term for homosexuals in the USA)! It has taken me a long time to realise that they are not being offensive or rude.'

As part of their entry requirements to higher education, international students have to satisfy different tests of their language ability, both verbal and written. Notwithstanding, previous English language learning only partially prepares students for the total impact of a new language, twenty-four hours per day, every day.

Within the context of counselling, language is the most regular vehicle through which understanding is pursued. When a client's or counsellor's competence in the language they use in the counselling process is not high, then a potentially difficult scenario is set for misunderstanding.

An African student was referred to a student counsellor by a doctor in the health service who rang the counsellor and explained the reason for the referral. Apparently the student had visited the health service several times during the last few weeks complaining about his head itching. The doctor had checked for lice, nits, dandruff, drying skin, indeed anything that would cause irritation. Nothing was found. The student continued to complain. Only in discussing this case with medical colleagues over coffee was any light thrown on the matter by a doctor who had lived and worked in the same part of Africa as the student some years previously. She remembered that this was a way of saying 'I am worried' or 'I am depressed'.

Needless to say, metaphors, sayings and symbols are also subject to different interpretations. Student counsellors may have to employ additional methods to ensure their accuracy in understanding international students. These might include, for example:

1 the use of drawings/symbols created by the client or provided by the counsellor, as a basis for further discussion or/and as a different medium for communication;
2 extending the length of time of the interviews;
3 using an official translator;
4 involving an appropriate friend or student from the same country who has greater linguistic capacity;
5 referring the student to another counsellor with greater linguistic ability and/or knowledge of the cultural background of the student.

DISCRIMINATION, STEREOTYPING AND RACISM

Sadly, international students can become the focus of discrimination, stereotyping and racism from both within and outside the educational institution.

Academic and other staff may themselves be discriminatory towards international students in a whole variety of ways, from insensitivity in the use of unfamiliar names to ill-conceived stories that communicate negative attitudes, from non-verbal behaviours that are disrespectful to systematically giving lower marks.

There can be occasional acts of racism on campus, against individuals and sometimes against groups. Graffiti, intimidation, violence and bullying may all be perpetrated by fellow students and others. International students also report that such negative behaviours towards them are often displayed by persons in the community at large, in theatres, shops, on buses and so on. The experience of such hostility can be the cause of considerable psychological and emotional distress for international students and could ultimately lead to dropping out or exam failure.

The student counsellor may be one of the people to whom the victimised student may turn for support. It is absolutely crucial, in our opinion, that counsellors, through training, have examined their own assumptions and attitudes in relation to these issues. A more extended consideration of these issues and how they relate to counselling can be found in the books by Dryden *et al.* (1989) and D'Ardenne and Mahtani (1989).

BEYOND THE INDIVIDUAL: IMPLICATIONS FOR THE COUNSELLOR

Beyond dealing with individual students, the student counsellor is also in a position to stimulate the development of policy guidelines, contribute to staff training programmes and be supportive of anti-discriminatory initiatives in the students' union. Pressure of space has precluded us from dealing with these issues specifically, but readers will find a range of initiatives that student counsellors become involved in, by virtue of their preventative and developmental roles, in the following two chapters.

The two following sections, however, on peer-pairing and reorientation, are included as specific examples of very appropriate group-work that can be conducted with international students. Other group-work initiatives will also include orientation programmes, dealing with culture shock, home student/ international student links, introductions to studying in Britain, dealing with British culture, language skills, practice in groups and so on.

PEER-PAIRING

These schemes are designed to assist international students to settle down in their new place of study. Simply, a structure is created whereby a volunteer UK student is paired with an international student with the intention of providing friendly support. 'Befriending' schemes such as this have enormous potential though, of course, there can also be difficulties.

In a scheme launched at Sheffield University some years ago, over one hundred volunteers came forward to assist. This group were given a day and a half's training to help them prepare for their task. Their training included basic helping skills, cross-cultural awareness and ideas for 'joint activities'. Up to two volunteers were placed with groups of four or five international students. Same-gender pairings were maintained, thus avoiding the potentially complex area of culturally different expectations of different-gender relationships.

The task of the home volunteers was to offer general and social opportunities for international students to begin to feel at home in their new place of study. Modifications to this first course have continued and different schemes on language support and social interaction have now been developed to suit the local conditions at Sheffield.

REORIENTATION

Helping international students prepare to return to their home countries can seem, at first, an unusual project to embark upon. However, stimulated by some activity on this theme in Canada, the United Kingdom Council for Overseas Student Affairs (UKCOSA) published an article some years ago upon the ideas behind reorientation programmes. These courses are still very few and far between, but nevertheless, the thinking behind them has attracted some attention.

What is often not recognised by many colleges is the effect of 'secondary culture-shock', the psychological and emotional phenomena that occur when students return to their home countries. The common sense assumption is that, in returning home, people will immediately feel 'at home'. Research and many personal experiences demonstrate that this is not so.

Returning students often report being treated as an outsider or 'foreigner' upon their return home. Their families may not want to hear of their travels and experiences abroad, may accuse them of putting on 'airs and graces' and generally relate to them differently than before. To go home and to feel that it is not the same home as remembered can be most upsetting.

In short, reorientation programmes try to assist students in the anticipation and preparation for their return. A workshop of perhaps just one afternoon might prove of immense value in contributing to this process. Indeed, such courses could also prove to be of immense assistance to many home students, and the collaboration of counsellors with colleagues from careers, academic and other departments could provide this valuable addition to the overall learning programme.

DISCUSSION ISSUES

1 What are the similarities and differences that exist between the culture shock process and other transition phases, e.g. job loss, homesickness, etc.?
2 What are some major differences between the behaviour of people from different cultures?
3 How does British culture affect the approach to study employed by British colleges and universities?
4 Try to identify any specific skills required by student counsellors for dealing competently with international students.

Part III

WORK BEYOND THE COUNSELLING ROOM

6

The Counselling Service and the Implications of its Relationship with Others

INTRODUCTION

This section of the book focuses on the work of the counsellor outside the counselling room. All three chapters extol the value of taking a wider 'community work' and educational perspective.

In this chapter we will be considering the relationship between the counsellor and the wide variety of people who may, from time to time, seek contact for specific purposes. Whilst the counsellors' role is one that has, at heart, a wish to be helpful to people, it is also necessary to be aware of how that work is perceived by others and the implications this will have for dealing with those others.

The following sections detail specific aspects of these outside relationships that require consideration and ongoing monitoring.

LIAISON AND CONSULTANCY WITH STAFF

In general, student counsellors are delighted to be invited in to speak at departmental and faculty meetings. Such opportunities allow them to meet other staff (many colleges now have very large staff numbers, making personal contacts much harder) and provide a unique chance to talk about the work of the counselling service as well as listen to the professional concerns of colleagues.

Academic staff, inevitably, through their tutorial work, come across student problems. Meetings such as mentioned above afford the staff member an opportunity to discuss these case examples. If the student counsellor, through their presence and their contribution to the dilemmas raised, is able to offer support, ideas and guidance to the tutors concerned then not only may the individual troubled student be helped by the tutor but a wider opportunity for the dissemination of counselling knowledge has also been given to tutors. They can be helped to understand the need for and skills of referral. Where a student is happy to be helped and supported by a tutor, but refuses to be referred elsewhere, the counsellor can advertise the fact that they are happy to be used as a consultant by tutors. What the student counsellor does in meetings with academic staff can thus be a mixture of training, liaison and consultancy. Indeed some counsellors offer a regular support/case meeting for any staff in the college who regularly help students.

Despite the very positive tenor in which the above paragraphs have been written, several delicate and complex areas of professional and ethical procedure need always to be borne in mind by the counsellor. An ill-considered response or an indiscretion of name or subject matter might have far-reaching effects, not only upon clients but also upon counsellors themselves.

CONFIDENTIALITY

Confidentiality remains at the core of ethical and professional practice in counselling. Those who use the counselling service and the concerns they bring are matters that are kept confidential between the counsellor and client.

Similarly, when counsellors meet academic colleagues in a group, the counsellor will urge them (1) to respect confidentiality within the group, so that information does not leak outside indiscriminately and (2) to be prudent about the use of names of students they are helping. In most circumstances, the tutor requires help with the issues raised by the 'case' and does not need to divulge the name, which might affect the attitude of other tutors at the meeting towards that student.

Sometimes staff members may want to know about the progress being made by a student they have referred or may want to check that someone has turned up for counselling when they have recommended it.

There are different beliefs amongst student counsellors about divulging this 'attendance' issue. Is the attendance itself a matter of confidentiality between the client and the counselling service or is it only the issues that have been discussed that are confidential?

The tutor's genuine concern, conveyed by the enquiry, is not doubted. Nevertheless, they might best be helped by asking why they themselves cannot ask the student about attendance and progress. The very fact that they have referred the student means that they already know of the client's difficulty. However, tutors are often reluctant to address the issue again with the student, perhaps because of a wish not to enquire too closely into others' difficulties or to invade others' privacy. Finding out through a third party (the counsellor) seems an easier way to do it, especially if the tutor also does not trust the student's response. The counsellor, however, whilst not wishing to denigrate the tutor's concern or sense of responsibility, has to be very clear where they draw the line on what is confidential.

Rather more difficult to deal with can be the apparently innocent enquiry made during a social conversation, perhaps at lunch or over coffee break. The desirability of counsellor involvement with others in the organisation has to be tempered by a certain vigilance to such issues, especially in informal situations where the counsellor considers they are 'off duty'. We would argue they are seldom off duty.

These issues are serious because the ethic of confidentiality is the operational basis for counselling. Once a matter has been divulged without the client's permission, the tutor (and his or her colleagues) might feel they can ask for information anytime, and importantly, they and all others who hear about such an indiscretion lose confidence both in the principles and professional practice of the service. Such a loss of public confidence will affect the way the service is seen and subsequently used, to everyone's detriment.

THE ADVOCACY ROLE OF THE COUNSELLOR

Sometimes the counsellor may be called upon to be an advocate for the student who has a difficulty of some kind with the administration. Counsellors in education in general are regularly asked by students to send letters on their behalf to examining boards or heads of department, explaining that they have had a valid reason for not attending or achieving lower grades than expected. Such letters can become the sole purpose of a student's attendance at a counselling service and the counsellor faces a difficult duty in being both honourable towards the client and to the institution. In this respect, the counsellor is being used as a rubber stamp to validate the 'truth' of a personal problem while, of course, being totally dependent on the client for the veracity of the story. Each counsellor has to judge for him or herself the value and importance of communication with departments over these matters and each may take a different approach to how they confront these requests. In further education colleges it is not uncommon for counsellors to be much more actively involved in advocacy work. For example, they may sit on committees which consider the special needs of students with disabilities or learning difficulties. Some counsellors also conduct intake interviews with students who may encounter particular difficulties and are instrumental in helping to identify problems and to work towards finding solutions with the student.

AVOIDING OVERLY SIMPLE ANSWERS AND OPINIONS

Conversations with friends, tutors or parents of clients can prove particularly 'sticky', especially when they are anxious or are asking very difficult (if not impossible) questions, e.g. 'When will they get better?', 'They are tipped for a good exam pass, can you treat their panic, quickly?', 'Just keep me informed of all developments and tell me what I should tell his mother.'

The counsellor is not being 'bloody-minded' or holding something back when they avoid overly simple answers and opinions to such questions. Rather, they are only too aware:

1   that human situations causing emotional and psychological upsets are often complex before they become simple;

2 that counselling, as a method of aiding the resolution of difficulties, is geared towards assisting the *exploration* of issues, not the *giving* of answers;

3 that counsellors, in their interaction with staff members (for complex reasons of institutional politics or a sense of closer colleagueship) might be drawn in to inappropriately supporting staff views of the student that are overly simplistic or 'judgemental';

4 that counsellors themselves, especially if they are extremely busy, might be tempted to short-circuit the exploratory process.

The counsellor's work with staff, friends and parents has several perspectives. The opportunity exists in the meeting between the two parties for the counsellor to act as a role model. By their way of being they can assist the other person to understand the value of respectful and exploratory responses. They can help the other person to clarify their position. The counsellor's refusal to be drawn into overly simple responses demonstrates the seriousness of consideration which they bring to the situations being described.

Of course, there are many situations in which offering reassurance and accurate information to people directly associated with the client can be of immense value. Examples of this might include details of specific mental illnesses (if the client has been diagnosed) or the possibility of repeat years or repeat exams in certain circumstances and so on. Accurate information can also be most reassuring.

The client's significant others can bring enormous personal pressure to bear on the counsellor to come up with resolutions. It is important that the counsellor can understand and recognise these pressures as indications of the pressure being experienced by such people in their helping roles.

CLARIFICATION OF RESPONSIBILITY

Under pressure, all of us can get into situations that in a calmer moment we would not have agreed to! Problems can arise for the counsellor and the tutor when they liaise, if insufficient care is taken in this process.

Tutors   can   coerce   counsellors   into   assuming   full responsibility for students (inappropriately), can dump the effects of less than adequate tutoring upon the counsellor and indeed generally blame the counsellor for not 'sorting out' the student. Counsellors can likewise blame tutors for being inadequate teachers, not having sufficient sensitivity to students and not assuming the appropriate authority their role demands.

When tutors and counsellors work together on behalf of the welfare of students, it is important that they spend sufficient time agreeing who does what, how and when.

As an example, after collaboration between the student, the tutor and the counsellor the following might be decided. The student agrees to work harder at deadlines. If this is not possible they may agree to submit their working drafts on the deadline date. The tutor agrees to mark and comment on these and continues to provide tutorial support. The counsellor, with the student's permission, might also write a formal note to the department indicating that at the present time the student, because of personal circumstances, is unable to operate at their best. (This point can also be helpful to the tutor, as an aid to their defence of the student at meetings where academic progress of students is reviewed.) In the meantime the counsellor will continue to work with the student on their personal difficulties.

COUNSELLORS: DISCIPLINARIANS AND AGENTS OF CONTROL?

Where clarification of responsibility fails, counsellors can become embroiled in and at worst made responsible for disciplinary procedures in colleges. A colleague in further education, upon our enquiry about this issue, volunteered immediately that disciplinary matters had always been dealt with by referring them to the counselling service. If a student's behaviour in a department had evoked a disciplinary response, they would be 'sent for counselling'. Inevitably, not only would that student arrive feeling resentful and resistant but the very purpose of the counselling service was altered.

Despite having attempted to resist this misuse of counselling, it was only since the appointment of a new head of student services in that college that this practice had been successfully challenged and individual academic departments charged with the task.

A counsellor in another college was sent a student who had caused a fight. The student had been told that they could continue on their course only if they saw the counsellor on a weekly basis. Counselling had been tied in to the institutional requirements, not the personal needs of the student.

One further example is worth quoting here. An academic department in a college 'successfully' recruited several students from a local young people's hostel. However, soon after the course started, staff became quite anxious about the apparent levels of disturbance being manifested by this small group. They were all sent to the counselling service!

In circumstances where such confusion over the counselling task has occurred the counsellors have been involved inappropriately by others 'because they deal with student problems' or 'because they can manage discipline with sensitivity' and other reasons containing rationalisations and misunderstandings. We would argue that it is quite inappropriate for counsellors to become involved, other than as 'witnesses', in the administration of disciplinary procedures. All three examples given above see the use of counselling as an agency of control; the anxiety of the various academic staff has converted the counselling service into a depository for all difficult students and situations.

The counsellor who becomes associated with disciplinary procedures is in grave danger of losing the unique occupational territory they occupy within the organisation. Any member of the institution may consult them confidentially and expect to have that confidence maintained. However, students and staff will think twice before consulting a counsellor who is too closely associated with institutional authority and power. Trust in the counsellor's capacity to manage the complex boundaries between confidentiality and institutional responsibility will be sorely stretched in the eyes of students if such referrals go on unchallenged!

In many smaller colleges, where the counsellor might be better known personally and where a multiplicity of tasks are carried out by them, then the boundaries in which the counselling service operates will be less clear. Counsellors may have to work very hard to maintain their professional views and will require a sufficient degree of internal psychological security to deal with these unrealistic expectations.

POWER, ROLE AND OPPRESSION

All the above points and the scenarios they present have the complex dimensions of power, role confusion and oppression embedded in them. We do not wish to overstate this arena of difficulty but counsellors do need to be sensitive to it.

Counsellors can be subject to the whims of senior management, to the excesses of inappropriate decisions made by those in power and exposed to the consequences such decisions will create. They need to walk what can only be described as a tightrope existence in their various dealings with others. Their job is unique in the organisation, and demands that they are able to occupy the uncomfortable hinterland between being an 'insider' and an 'outsider'. If they become too involved with institutional politics, procedures and practices, too involved in relationships with senior staff and committees, they might become overly identified with the aims of the organisation. On the other hand, consequences can also exist for the counselling practitioners (and possibly their clients) who attempt to remain neutral and aloof from the organisation.

Crucially, the counsellor has to be aware of not being oppressed by or oppressing others, staff and students. There are times when they will have to exercise their personal power against those wielding institutional power. They will also have to, from time to time, protect against any inappropriate erosion and change of their roles by others.

For example, a long-serving member of staff (15 years) was referred by her manager to the counsellor. Her work had apparently been deteriorating. The manager's final words in the referring phone call were 'see her, let me know what you think, keep me informed. I can arrange any specific courses or leave of absence for her that you recommend.' The counsellor's response to this final statement was to indicate the confidentiality of the counselling process and to point out to the manager that they would only contact him should the client give permission.

The client attended for counselling reluctantly, having been told to! She would not have come otherwise. Yes, she had been depressed recently and indeed had seen her doctor. There had been a considerable number of changes in her department and she was not happy with the implications of these in terms of their impact upon students. She had begun to feel she no longer fitted in. She could not see how counselling could help and did not want another appointment but was grateful for the counsellor's concern. The counsellor asked her if she wanted him to say anything to the manager. She said she was already scheduled to meet the manager when she got back from holidays so she would talk to him herself.

Three weeks went by. The manager rang the counselling service, complaining that no information about the client had been sent to him. As the manager had to decide whether or not to sack the client (a long way from the first phone call of offered help and training) would the counsellor please let him know what to do?

As an aside, the above scenario demonstrates the wisdom of the question 'Who is complaining?' Counsellors can sometimes become embroiled in complex dynamics that can confuse their own sense of purpose. The manager is complaining. It is the manager who is seeking help from the counsellor as to what to do about the member of staff. Unfortunately the manager would never be likely to consult the counsellor personally. The counsellor in this situation was aware that he was being inappropriately used by the manager. He was experiencing considerable pressure and stress and now felt caught between a very real concern for the client and the dominating nature of the manager's demand.

Because of the circumstances, he took the very unusual step of contacting the staff member and openly explaining his own dilemma. As it was now several weeks later many changes could have occurred to the client and he didn't feel able or willing to communicate out-of-date information but indicated that the manager was still requiring it from him. The client brought the counsellor up to date with present circumstances and gave her permission to communicate what he felt was right to the manager concerned. At no time did the client realise that her own job was apparently under threat.

Taking the various elements into account (and having discussed this situation fully with his supervisor) the counsellor decided to write a letter to the manager that (1) acknowledged the manager's difficulties in this situation, (2) recognised a general lift in the client's morale since the holiday, (3) explained the nature and importance of confidentiality in counselling and (4) talked about the difficulties generally related to job stress and how managers can be supportive to employees. A final paragraph was also appended indicating the client's commitment to her job and the importance attributed to the supportive nature of the manager's task. In this way the counsellor considered that he had acted ethically with both parties concerned; moreover the importance of his role and ethical practice had been crucially maintained.

Much more attention needs to be devoted to these difficult facets of the student counsellor's occupation than we have been able to give it here. However, we hope that we have included enough material above to afford readers an insight into these operational complexities that underlie the counselling role in education.

DISCUSSION ISSUES

1 It is acknowledged that ethical practice is of paramount importance in all professions. Why are questions of ethical practice so pertinent to the task of student counselling?
2 What steps might the student counsellor take to ensure that their role is understood by members of the college community?

7

Preventative Work

INTRODUCTION: CONTRIBUTIONS TO THE LEARNING ENVIRONMENT

Beyond the domain of counselling individuals, the Association for Student Counselling has always maintained the view that counsellors also need to work in preventative and developmental ways within the college environment. Inevitably some overlap will exist between what is considered to be developmental and preventative.

This chapter seeks to focus on that facet of the counsellor's work that contributes to enhancing the quality of students' lives whilst they are in college. Enabling students (1) to settle down well, (2) to learn to study efficiently, (3) to manage personal difficulties and experience development in groups and (4) to help themselves are all activities that fall within this preventative role.

Using the caveat that 'prevention is better than cure', counsellors may work towards equipping students with the necessary 'tools' to manage the educational experience more successfully by themselves and in co-operation with others. It makes sound educational sense that young people are assisted in their developmental processes in a natural and structured way rather than through negative personal circumstances and stresses eventually requiring counselling.

Work with students in this chapter is broadly divided into four areas:

1   the development of confidence and knowledge, through orientation programmes;
2   the acquisition of academic skills;

3 promotion of short courses and workshops to assist students in specific problem areas, e.g. the management of anxiety, eating disorders, etc.;
4 helping students to help themselves.

In all of the above activities the counsellor is attempting to address the overall needs of all students. Sadly, of course, the volume of student numbers in the majority of further and higher educational settings means that the counsellor may only be able to touch the tip of the iceberg with their work. However many courses they run, they will not be able to reach every student. This obvious reality invites the counsellor to explore ways and means of encouraging staff to understand the need for and acquire the necessary skills and knowledge in these activities so that a greater majority of the student population benefits from them. The next chapter therefore offers further ideas on staff development.

ORIENTATION PROGRAMMES: THE DEVELOPMENT OF CONFIDENCE IN AND KNOWLEDGE OF THE INSTITUTION

During the last ten years very interesting research evidence has emerged from the United States on the importance of helping students into college life. Historically, the American higher education system has experienced higher levels of student withdrawal or delays in degree completion than in the United Kingdom. In part, these factors have been an accepted facet of this very different system.

Nevertheless, American educationists were concerned to understand the reasons why students withdrew in such numbers. A critical finding was the huge impact upon students made by the transition from home to the place of study.

Mention has already been made in Chapter 3 of the disorientating effects of this transitional process and Shirley Fisher's work on homesickness has provided substantial evidence of the manner in which these concerns manifest themselves.

From a developmental and preventative perspective, the counsellor's role can be seen as one of contributing (if at all possible) to creating the conditions in the institution in which learning can occur. Indeed, it could be argued that unless these conditions are present then the task of acquiring new knowledge becomes formidable.

What are the conditions we are talking about? Well, for a start, an individual needs to feel welcomed into a new environment. They also need to know a range of data about their living accommodation and their courses of study. With regards to accommodation this will include very basic knowledge of meal-times, security arrangements, where messages can be left, who the person in charge is, what the important rules of the house are and so on.

They need to be helped, through formal and informal means, to establish friendly contact with other students, both in their accommodation and on their course. Courses can assist in these processes by designing class activities that bring groups together for discussion or projects. Indeed, inventive projects such as taking the students into locations around the campus and into the local community will also assist in helping students find their way around in a strange town.

In a previous college one of the authors worked in, a department designed a two-week orientation course for their students, which went most satisfactorily. The numbers of course withdrawals at the end of that academic year were significantly lower than previous years where an orientation course had not existed. Interestingly, a year later, because of revised timetables and pressures to include new academic demands, the orientation course was reduced to three days. The result? The withdrawal rate increased again!

What has all this to do with the student counsellor? They are but one person in the college. They have no direct power over teaching timetables. They cannot enforce the creation of orientation programmes and they certainly don't have the resources to run them. In fact there is a terrible feeling that they can do very little.

What they do have to offer, however, is the knowledge of the importance of a good psychological and emotional climate for students to work well. Equipped with this knowledge they are able, in their contacts with staff, to stimulate thought and offer ideas and support for orientation initiatives. What the counsellor is able to do will depend upon the local circumstances they find themselves in. Membership of strategic committees, good working relationships with specific academic departments, stimulating the formation of a small working party and writing a paper for discussion are all methods through which the counsellor may help focus attention upon this crucial phase of the educational process.

Following recent government policy there has been a very substantial increase in the student population in recent years. The speed of this expansion has not been matched by the provision of appropriate resources. The differential nature of these two factors may well lead to an increase in student withdrawal rates in the next few years. Appropriate orientation programmes for all students may assist the retention rates and (more appropriately from a counselling perspective), ensure that students are helped to manage the transition process.

THE ACQUISITION OF ACADEMIC SKILLS

Study skills

The counsellor in higher and further education may be concerned with the study-related problems of individual clients but may also wish to inform the academic staff of the role of emotion and experience in the creation and overcoming of study-related problems. As we have mentioned elsewhere, it is wise to bear in mind that our very earliest experiences of learning occurred when we were small children and took place within the context of the child–parent relationship. When academic work goes badly wrong, the student may be overwhelmed by feelings that seem to have little relation to the rather mundane task in hand. Learning and studying are not simply intellectual activities but involve emotional experience.

Counsellors may also initiate or encourage teaching staff to set up specific courses on study skills for a range of students who may have been educated along quite different lines or who have been out of the education process for decades or who simply need to be helped to adapt to the institution's style of delivering education. The more specific the study skills, the more use students can make of the enterprise.

Where counsellors may have to provide study skills training themselves, recourse to a wide range of literature on the subject is possible. There is also a role for relaxation training in improving concentration as is mentioned under the section on exam skills.

The greatest resource in teaching study skills is the student group itself. The authors have found that whenever they have organised study and exam-related workshops, individuals come up with surprising and innovative ways in which to tackle problems. Similarly another important part of the workshops always appears to be the opportunity for students to explore, in a safe environment, their feelings and thoughts about themselves, about academic pressure and the positions they and their families adopt *vis-à-vis* academic achievement.

Exam skills

There are three aspects to worries related to exams which may usefully be considered separately. Firstly, some students may have trouble preparing themselves realistically in terms of revision technique. This is commonly a cause for apprehension in students who have not recently taken academic exams and who may have difficulty in restricting their scope for revision. Others may have kept poor notes or have missed a lot of classes.

Secondly, students may be well equipped to prepare themselves but be less able to perform to their own satisfaction. Again, this may be due to lack of practice or lack of training in exam technique. Where a student is dyslexic and has been diagnosed formally he or she will be entitled to special dispensations in the exam. Help with structuring revision timetables and guidelines on appropriate areas of revision are evidently important to discuss. Sometimes exam technique itself needs some attention, with opportunities for timed essays or attempts to make notes on past papers. A variety of excellent books are available as guides to good exam practice. Generally speaking, students know a lot about exam skills and how to revise, but for a variety of reasons do not use this knowledge. Individual counselling is frequently about exploring the meanings of this refusal to benefit from what the client knows.

The third kind of exam worry, falling completely to pieces in the exam itself and dread of this phenomenon, is another issue which is regularly brought to the attention of counsellors rather than academics.

A gentle enquiry into the feelings and thoughts stirred up by exams can be revealing. Frequently, the capacity of the counsellor and client to talk through the feelings and thoughts which are aroused is sufficient, in itself, to help the client approach the exams in a more effective manner. However, there are other, more active ways of helping students with exam anxiety which some counsellors may wish to use or to recommend.

Practical help for exam nerves

In his paper, 'Examination anxiety: what the student counsellor can do', Windy Dryden found that students who knew they would have difficulty with 'nerves' did well if they commenced a course of relaxation training some time before they were due to sit exams. The relaxation helped not only with staying in control in the exam situation but also improved revision and recall in the period before the exam. There are several ways in which students can find opportunities to learn relaxation techniques. They can join regular relaxation groups, which counsellors or other colleagues may set up, or they can enrol on yoga courses or buy relaxation tapes commercially or from the counselling service if resources exist to pay for such items. Tutors can play a helpful role in encouraging the student to start such training well in advance of exams.

If there is a need, a referral can then be made to the counselling service for more individual help. The General Practitioner may also be willing to prescribe appropriate medication if self-help techniques founder or there is not time to spare. Very anxious students may have to sit exams in a room on their own, with academic colleagues supervising their progress. Where student health clinics exist, they often provide this caretaking function at times of special stress.

WORKING WITH STUDENT GROUPS ON SPECIFIC PROBLEM ISSUES

Anxiety management and relaxation training

The incidence of anxiety-related difficulties in the population as a whole is quite high. Student populations often reflect similar percentages of distress in this regard. In reviewing the annual statistics of one university counselling service, the authors found that anxiety-related difficulties came fourth in a list of central presenting problems of clients. Approximately 10 per cent of the clients had presented with this condition (43 individual clients).

Suspecting that there might be quite a few more persons suffering similarly in the student community the counsellors thought that they would advertise a short course, comprising five sessions of one-and-a-half hours each, on the management of anxiety. Colleagues in other student services were informed (e.g. health service, careers service, chaplaincy, accommodation and welfare provision) as were some tutorial and residential staff. Short announcements were also placed in the staff newsletter and the students' union newspaper.

As a result, thirty applications were received, some as referrals through the health service. Each applicant was offered a brief interview in which their reasons for coming could be explained a little and at the same time the counsellors could describe how they envisaged the course would run.

Given the high number of applications the group was divided into two separate groups, run at different times in the term. Unlike some other previous group-work initiatives the counsellors had been involved in, there was a maximum dropout of only two people over the five weeks of each course. The counsellors concerned believe that a significant cause of this high retention rate was the initial interview, which afforded the opportunity for the students to meet the counsellors and share their particular concerns in relation to anxiety. In return the counsellors, having met the students and heard their stories, were able to reassure them in their predicament and allow for any specific anxieties raised within the overall course design.

A fairly structured course was designed, with clear times for starting and ending, and guidelines discussed on confidentiality, smoking and a general plea for sensitivity to each other's concerns. Members were reassured that they would not have to speak in or to the whole group unless they so chose. Suffice to say that a course on managing anxiety must not create anxiety!

During the course of the five sessions the participants were introduced to a series of different ideas and strategies for helping themselves. They were also given an account of how anxiety and stress affect our bodies (physiological response, panic attacks, sweating, palpitations, etc.) as well as our thoughts, our feelings and our behaviour.

Each week was devoted to a different aspect and during the time allotted some points or theory would be offered, followed by activities (questionnaires, group discussions in twos and fours, co-counselling, relaxation exercises) and sometimes finishing with the group being asked to try out a 'homework' task on the subject.

Comments made by course members afterwards indicated that many had benefited from the course in a variety of ways, some of which they could not have anticipated. Sharing with others and realising they were not 'the only ones' was of immense help, as was the support they experienced from each other. Several participants also reported that the course had helped them in their relationships with other people and most pertinently, in dealing with the situations that had formerly been anxiety-provoking.

HELPING STUDENTS HELP THEMSELVES

Other group-work

From time to time, tutors may invite the student counsellor to run a workshop with a class of students, as part of their coursework. The authors have been involved in running workshops with education and social work students on counselling skills, for example, or with art therapy students on the impact of race and culture upon therapy.

This category is one in which the counsellor is being explicitly invited into the teaching domain to offer their particular skills and expertise.

Ready-formed groups of students may come together through a shared concern, worry or a matter of mutual interest and approach a counsellor for help. A specific example would be where a group of students, possibly postgraduates, have recognised their anxiety at the prospect of having to give a seminar on their research and turn to the student counsellor to seek assistance on this task. An agreement may be reached that the counsellor assists them in aspects of presentation skills, public speaking, psychological and physical preparation before the seminar and so on.

What other sorts of course might the counsellor become involved with? Inevitably different emphases and patterns of practice emerge in different institutions, often reflecting the nature of the student community, contemporary issues of concern and the levels of knowledge, skill and interest of individual counsellors. Student counsellors have, at different times, run courses for groups on the following topics:

1   making friends;
2   confidence building;
3   eating problems (anorexia and bulimia);
4   dealing with sexuality;
5   social skills;
6   dealing with drink and drugs;
7   homesickness and other transitions;
8   bereavement;
9   co-operative team work;
10 issues of culture and race for home and international students.

Obviously, very few counsellors could mount such a broad range of courses as an expert on each subject. However, counsellors do have the skills of facilitating groups and often have many contacts upon whom they can also call for assistance. Part of their task will be to encourage the group to take responsibility to pursue appropriate learning, providing information where necessary; but most importantly the counsellor will assist the group to function in a spirit of co-operation, openness and mutual enquiry.

Training volunteer students from student societies

Student life is enriched by the existence of numerous societies which students set up out of interest or to further their needs politically or socially or in connection with religious or sporting aspirations. Many student societies play a useful role in creating a sympathetic and facilitative climate for people who may have cause to feel particularly anxious or unsupported. 'Nightline' is a student organisation with independent groups across the country which aims to provide a telephone helpline to any student who would like to speak to anyone about anything, from finding out the time of the last bus home to disclosing depressed feelings about loneliness and self-worth. 'Nightliners' arrange training in listening skills and telephone skills and may call on student counsellors, amongst others, to help them in this endeavour. At times, there are complex matters (e.g. masturbatory phone calls, suicide thoughts, overinvolvement of volunteers) which arise from telephone-line work which 'Nightliners' may also need to explore in further training sessions. Counsellor liaison with organisations such as 'Nightline' can be a valuable way of spreading communication skills and psychological understanding into the student population in a non-stigmatising fashion.

Other societies, for example gay, lesbian and bisexual societies, if they exist, may also call on counsellors to assist them in training volunteers to be available during 'awareness' campaigns to respond to people enquiring about the societies' activities. Enquiries during campaigns need to be handled sensitively and listening and facilitating skills can greatly enhance the ability of respondents to carry out their tasks effectively and to learn skills which may be of lifelong value.

All of the work that is carried out with different societies needs also to address the ethical issues involved as well as questions of confidentiality and ground rules about appropriate behaviour. Notions about acceptable boundaries can vary enormously from person to person and although such differences cannot be legislated against, there can be useful debates about the implications, for example, of getting intimately involved with someone who has come to you in the first instance for information and advice.

Providing training to student societies can be an efficient use of time for counsellors, in that it strengthens contacts and deepens understanding for students and counsellors alike, which may well benefit both parties, especially where referral is necessary. In Chapter 8, we outline the kind of activities likely to be covered in a six-week introduction to counselling skills course. Some of those activities lend themselves remarkably well to the kind of brief listening-skills training outlined above.

DISCUSSION ISSUES

1 Can you think of other subject areas beyond those already considered in the chapter that might prove of value to students?

2 What do you think that clients of the counsellor might feel if they then met him or her running a student group that they joined? What might be the implications for both?

8

Staff Training and Development

A RATIONALE FOR COUNSELLOR INVOLVEMENT IN STAFF TRAINING

Student counsellors may contribute to the appropriate support and training of other staff in the organisation by running short courses for lecturing staff on personal tutoring skills for example, or offering possibilities for groups of staff to meet with a counsellor to discuss issues in relation to 'problem' students.

Why is this dimension of a counsellor's work desirable in an educational environment?

Previous training. The counsellor, by virtue of their original training and later ongoing professional development, will have been exposed to a range of thought and experience about inter-personal relations, group dynamics and processes of learning. These experiences provide them with specific knowledge that can be most usefully shared with colleagues.

Direct professional experience. The counsellor's role offers them the opportunity of 'witnessing' students' accounts of their experience both as people and as participants in the college system. They are in possession, then, of a range of data that the institution might benefit from. (Please note that this does not mean that the counsellor breaks confidentiality in crudely presenting case studies, for example; rather that the essence of counselling work with students may be distilled in order to share the common threads of recurring patterns.)

Commitment to a conducive environment. Most often, the counsellor's work is focused upon individuals and their own difficulties. However, from time to time, a series of individual clients presenting similar stories may alert the counsellor to a 'pathology' (a system that is causing difficulties) within the college or specific department. Of course, after resolving the ethical issues involved, the counsellor may give direct feedback to that part of the institution that seems to be employing procedures that are not conducive to student learning. However the counsellor might also use the vehicle of staff training as a way of alerting staff, in general, to the consequences of their systems, policy and practice.

Efficiency. As stated elsewhere in the book, the size of counselling services in most colleges is relatively small, sometimes comprising only one staff member. Staff development courses offer opportunities for establishing contact with colleagues, sharing ideas, offering skills practice and in many other ways impacting upon the whole system. More informed and sensitive work with students by colleagues might, in part, prevent situations from deteriorating to the point where students request individual counselling. It is efficient for the institution as well as the counsellor to spread both skills and knowledge.

INTRODUCTION TO COUNSELLING SKILLS

Many teaching, administrative and support staff have occasional experiences of students (and sometimes colleagues) turning to them for help when they are upset or troubled in some way. One of the most obvious and most apt courses for counsellors to run, then, is an introduction to the skills of counselling.

There are a variety of 'training' resources available to help counsellors prepare appropriate courses. Details of these may be obtained through enquiry to the British Association for Counselling (see also Inskipp 1986).

With relatively short time-spans in which to fit important concepts of learning and practice, the counsellor as trainer is faced with difficult decisions as to the appropriate content of such courses. Inevitably, the content will be different depending upon each trainer's theoretical orientation and the trainees' expressed needs. A broad outline of one such course is given below as an example.

87

On Listening and Learning

Example of a course outline

Course duration: six sessions of three hours.
Course participants: any member of the college staff who has to use counselling skills from time to time.
Training group size: eight to fifteen. This can depend upon the counsellor's comfort in working with different size groups, the number wishing to attend, the size of the training room(s) and whether a co-trainer is available.

Session 1: What is counselling?
This session would aim to set the scene for the course, and explore definitions of counselling and the implications these may have for the participants.

Session 2: Getting started
Included in this session would be a consideration of the creation of an appropriate climate for counselling, an exploration of the implications of non-verbal behaviour, the use of different response styles and possibly the introduction of a simple counselling model.

Session 3: How can I help when I am with the client?
Introduction to and practice of listening, use of open-ended questions, reflections, paraphrasing, picking up feelings – attending to the client's agenda.

Session 4: The concept of empathy
Introduction to the concept of empathy.
Role-play practice and discussion of issues.

Session 5: Challenges and difficulties for the helper
Dealing with helper's own feelings and thoughts.
Coping with client expression of feelings. Implications for the helper.
Further role-play practice and discussion.

Session 6: Summing up, referrals and endings
The limits to helping – what can I do and when should I refer?
Ideas and skills of referral.
Issues of ethical practice.
Dealing with boundaries and endings.
Final discussion.

COURSES ON PERSONAL TUTORING

At the time of writing, the concept of personal tutoring is under considerable pressure. As student numbers rapidly expand in the further and higher education sectors and academic staff also experience pressure to implement and publish research, less and less time is available for them to devote to personal tutoring tasks. Notwithstanding this, many individual staff are profoundly concerned to improve their personal tutorial skills with students. They recognise the importance of real contact between students and staff and how it can be helpful in assisting students through difficult periods of study and in their personal lives.

An outline of a one-afternoon course is given below as an example of the way in which counsellors can contribute:

1. introduction to course;
2. personal tutoring – exploring definitions – what is it?
3. exploration of the skills required;
4. possible use of video of a tutorial for discussion (Rickenson 1991);
5. departmental systems for tutoring (sharing out the work, different models, etc.);
6. discussion on the implications of confidentiality and complexities imposed upon academic judgement in helping situations;
7. skills of referral and knowledge of the other agencies.

Some counselling services also publish small booklets on personal tutoring for distribution to new staff. Such booklets can provide helpful hints and tips on the tutoring process as well as listing the welfare resources available to students. These can be used most effectively in conjunction with tutor training.

THE SKILLS OF WORKING WITH GROUPS

Given the present expansion of student numbers and an increasing interest in group approaches to learning, the student counsellor is well positioned to offer appropriate short course training to academic staff in this area. The overall concept of working with groups can of course also be extended to managing staff teams, working in committees and so on. All have, as their basis, the challenge of teaching or contributing productively to the combined output of and relationships between a group of people.

Self-evidently and perhaps a little perversely, the student counsellor may feel under considerable pressure, whilst running courses on this subject, to provide a good role model of group worker. The psychological pressure can prove to be a great hindrance to the trainer. However, the counsellor's sensitivity to their own discomfort is a very useful reminder of the daily strains incurred by teaching staff in managing difficult group situations.

As in counselling, there are different theoretical positions used to understand group-work processes. It is most important, therefore, for the counsellor/trainer to be comfortable with the underlying concepts of any course design they produce.

Different aspects may be featured, then, according to the chosen theoretical approach, and might include some of the following:

1 the establishment of introductory group exercises (e.g. 'pyramids' – using pairs, fours, eights for discussions);
2 the establishment of goals for the group;
3 the importance of boundaries and setting of group climate, staff–student contracts;
4 the functions of role and authority within groups;
5 the study of relationship patterns in groups;
6 what happens to communication in groups?
7 the implications of the group environment upon atmosphere, co-operation, productivity, etc. (seating, temperature, surroundings, etc.);
8 consideration of student experience in groups;
9 dealing with difficult group members;
10 the skills of facilitation.

As with the other courses mentioned in this chapter, it can be seen that assisting tutorial staff to work more skilfully and sensitively with groups of students will be directly contributing to the overall impact of the educational experience upon the students.

TRAINING STAFF IN HALLS OF RESIDENCE

All the old and new universities and colleges of higher education have considerable numbers of students in halls of residence. There are also some colleges of further education that provide residential facilities. In addition to the obvious staff who work in these settings (e.g. porters, security, cleaning staff, catering staff) there are often appointments of hall or resident tutors. These days the occupants of such posts may in the main be younger academics or postgraduate students. Their responsibilities are normally for specific areas or corridors of the hall of residence (where they might also live) as well as generally being responsible figures of authority in the hall in the warden's absence.

Because they work in the environment in which students are living, all staff in halls of residence have a key role to play in providing a user-friendly, homely environment. Reference was made, in Chapter 3, to these considerable difficulties created by homesickness. Many institutions have a policy of attempting to provide the maximum amount of their housing stock for first-year students. Manifestations of 'unhappiness' and 'unsettledness' can therefore be prevalent amongst the student body and appropriate emotional 'first aid' and support from staff can help prevent the situation from deteriorating further.

Student counsellors engaged in training hall tutors or other staff will often construct appropriate training courses around specific themes that have already been described in the previous sections. In short, the accent will be on assisting staff to recognise how best they can interact with students, individuals and groups: (1) to enable support and friendship networks to develop, (2) to act as appropriate sources of reference for students (for local knowledge, for spotting problems early, for explaining the college system, for being an 'old' hand) and (3) to be a symbol and figure of authority in the residential environment.

STRESS MANAGEMENT

A set of symptoms regularly presented by student and staff clients to counselling services are those related to stress. Some years ago one of the authors who had been invited to teach stress management to a youth and community work training course was asked by a secretary in that department if he could run such a course for her and her colleagues. The result was that, some weeks later, fifteen members of the secretarial and administrative staff attended a one-afternoon course. News apparently spread of this innovation and multiple requests led to further one-day courses (all full) being organised during the next two years for staff in the college!

A considerable range of books and audiotapes are now available to assist counsellors in designing these courses. A short programme could include the following activities:

1 exploring a definition of stress and how it affects human beings (e.g. mood, illness, impact upon thinking, decision-making, etc.);
2 exploring ways of spotting stress in ourselves and others – possible use of stress questionnaires;
3 a brainstorm to elicit the multiplicity of ways to help oneself deal with stress;
4 participants may be given an opportunity to experience breathing and relaxation exercises;
5 possible discussion of the value of diet, exercise, sleep, etc.

There is no doubt that many staff really value such an opportunity to be helped to contend with their stress levels. Sometimes, of course, staff may end up discussing aspects of their working environments that are stressful and to which there seems few possibilities of resolution. Occasionally this can be complicated in terms of institutional politics and it might be helpful for the staff member to be invited to discuss this phenomena with the counsellor elsewhere. Sometimes there can be very high levels of stress amongst staff who hold lower status in their organisation. They often feel they are not in a position to effect change very successfully. They are the ones who don't get consulted on policy or practice, get left out in terms of decision-making and so on. They can be in a particularly difficult position. Helping staff resolve and present their difficulties can be an important task for counsellors/trainers.

The counsellor also needs to keep in mind individual stress and the stress-producing effects of the institution as a whole. This factor is very similar to the counsellor's work with students. The institution itself might require challenging to change its harmful practices.

FURTHER CONSIDERATIONS ON STAFF DEVELOPMENT WORK BY STUDENT COUNSELLORS

The counsellor and the counselling service in any organisation can come to be seen as a symbolic safe container for institutional anxiety. The institution (comprising the staff who work in it) know that if problems erupt, then the counsellor can be consulted and the troubled person may, if willing, be referred.

This corporate projection upon the counsellor can weigh as a heavy burden upon the individual practitioner's shoulders. However, if the counsellor can accept this projection and recognise it for its symbolic quality (and not be driven by the expectation that they must cure everything – an impossibility anyway!) they will recognise that they have a certain element of power and institutional permission, as attributed by others, to initiate and facilitate staff training courses.

One of the frustrating difficulties facing counsellors can be the availability of staff to attend courses. Courses that require attendance over a period of time, during the working day, can produce difficulties for participants. Co-operation and good liaison with managers in the college is required to ensure that they will grant release to their employees to attend courses.

Working as a trainer with staff generally, many of whom may be very experienced lecturers, can prove quite anxiety-provoking for the counsellor. Often there can be great resistance on the part of the course participants to enter into the emotional domains raised by the training theme. Participation in group discussions and role-plays, for instance, can be resisted or dealt with only on a very intellectual level. The trainer's concern becomes how to manage the group climate in order to help the group explore the training issues from a balanced perspective of thinking and feeling, of being reflective and being more open.

In the first instance, if the counsellor is new to working as a trainer, it can be helpful to (1) conduct training in aspects of the work about which they are most knowledgeable and confident and (2) locate a colleague who can work as a co-trainer. It is obviously important that such a colleague is chosen for their compatibility, skill and knowledge. Working with someone one doesn't get along with can prove devastating to a course!

As an adjunct to staff training, counsellors may sometimes be invited in as consultants to departments to talk about their work or offer ideas on how best departments might consult them on matters of difficulty. These opportunities for consultation have a staff training dimension and provide good opportunities for 'educating' the community on the counsellor's domain of work.

Counsellors need to bring their listening capacities to bear in any of their contacts with staff in order to develop a deep understanding of their situation in relation to their training needs. In many instances these can be relayed on to the staff training units, where they exist, but sometimes the counsellor might choose to initiate training themselves.

Finally, if the counsellor, as trainer, can 'model' their training well, they offer participants an opportunity to experience first-hand the importance of a sensitive and clear working style that is conducive to personal learning. Research in education that was influenced by Carl Rogers' client-centred approach revealed how training course participants 'caught' experientially some of the valuable qualities in the teaching relationship from their trainers. Part of the anxiety of working as a trainer inevitably involves the burden of being such a role model!

DISCUSSION ISSUES

1 Student counsellors often operate under considerable pressure from individual students wishing to be seen for counselling. What sorts of rationales might they then develop, when they still choose to spend a certain amount of time doing staff training as opposed to seeing more individuals?

2 What particular knowledge, experience and skills do student counsellors have that makes their contribution to staff development a useful one?

3 Brainstorm other ideas for courses that student counsellors might organise for staff.

9

Concluding Thoughts

THE CHALLENGES OF STUDENT COUNSELLING

As authors, our constant challenge throughout the writing of this book has been how to condense the wide range of issues, counselling theories and models of practice prevalent in student counselling into an introductory text of this size. We hope that we have provided sufficient content and variety to inform and interest you, the reader. Our belief is that counsellors employed in further and higher education have an immensely important task to fulfil. They are in a unique position, through their training and through their clinical work with individuals, to inform and advise their educational colleagues and institutions on matters such as staff training, the psychology of learning and policy development.

The above paragraph perhaps might be seen to contain rather grandiose claims when placed alongside the all too often resource-starved, over-worked, stressed counsellor who cannot even counsel quickly enough to keep the waiting-list down! The newly-appointed student counsellor (who is often an isolated figure in an institution) is faced with the formidable task of establishing a pattern of professional work that combines clinical, preventative and developmental aspects that can be sustained over a long period of time. Too much work with individuals in trouble can prove immensely tiring and distressing. And if the counsellor becomes stressed their work is likely to deteriorate. Balancing this individual output with group and committee work, research or staff development can help the counsellor stay creative and affords opportunities to influence the educational climate in which students work.

The spectrum of counsellor activity that we have drawn in the preceding chapters certainly throws light upon the demands on and skills required of student counsellors. As people they require flexibility, stamina, personal confidence, psychological security and absolute discretion. With the current increases in student numbers and the lack of equivalent resourcing to meet client need, student counsellors are currently caught in a pincer movement between impossible numbers and expectations, on the one hand, and their wish to fulfil satisfactorily the aims of their professional task. An impossible equation.

CHALLENGES TO THE PROFESSIONALISM AND PERSONHOOD OF THE COUNSELLOR

In Chapters 3, 4 and 5 we introduced a range of issues and problem areas in life that are presented by clients to counselling services. In a busy week the counsellor might have anything between eighteen and twenty-five one-hour counselling sessions in which clients talk about the difficulties that concern them. (Please note that the Association for Student Counselling recommends that counsellors see between sixteen and twenty clients per week. Emergency situations and the sheer demand of waiting lists inevitably put pressures on the counsellor.) In just one week one of the authors saw four clients who had a background of child sexual abuse, two coping with lengthy and vitriolic parental divorce, a suicide attempt, a long-term bout of depression, three with serious anxiety problems and several others complaining of difficulties that they had already had for quite some time and could not resolve.

Counsellors working in the educational environment must be able to deal with other stresses too, such as the endings and losses and the strange pauses in continuity which breaks for vacations provide. The college or university is like a crucible with a constant flow of volatile material passing through every year. The counsellor may meet a student just once. That may be enough for the student to feel resolved and strengthened and to move on. Average numbers of counselling sessions per client can fluctuate between academic years and between different counsellors. However, a large proportion of student counselling is carried out over a period of one to six sessions.

Concluding thoughts

Despite the wide range of counselling theories, most acknowledge the importance of the creation of a relationship between counsellor and client as a basis for the therapeutic work. Inevitably, with longer-term clients, deeper relationships will be formed.

We can now see the counsellor as a person involved in a continuous round of intimate, sensitive relationships that are concentrated, demanding and intense. They can also be interrupted by vacations and frustrated by clients not continuing. Counsellors can be saddened and angered by aspects of the human condition they witness continually, and drained by the efforts such relationship-making and finishing demands. This means that the work is arduous and that counsellors need to take good care of themselves.

CONSULTANCY SUPPORT AND SUPERVISION

Based upon such a demanding scenario, it is professionally and personally incumbent upon the counsellor to ensure that they receive adequate consultancy support and supervision. The examples given above of the range of clients seen in just one week and the wear and tear of working in relationships gives an indication of how much the student counsellor needs support and structured reflective time to contemplate the effectiveness of their work.

Both the British Association for Counselling and the Association for Student Counselling now have Counsellor Accreditation Schemes and Policies for ethical practice which demand that counsellors have personal consultancy (or supervision as it has been traditionally known). These professional stipulations, combined with the envisaged influence of EC legislation upon the qualifications and licensing of counsellors and psychotherapists, means that counsellors will increasingly have to meet and fulfil such professional criteria.

Unfortunately, there are still college employers who are not sympathetic to these needs and do not, therefore, furnish the counsellor either with the time required (an hour weekly is recommended) or indeed pay the consultants' fees. Student counsellors in these circumstances have developed a range of methods to counter such institutional limitations. These include:

1 Finding a supervisor/consultant who provides their services free.

2 Establishing a reciprocal relationship with a colleague elsewhere, where each supervises the other, sharing the time equally.

3 Locating a group of colleagues from different organisations for group supervision. Each participant might contribute a small individual fee to the group, which, when combined with others, can be paid to a group supervisor. Alternatively, the group might appoint a 'rotating' supervisor from within its membership or decide between them to share the task. In both latter cases, there is no fee.

4 If permission for time off for supervision is withheld then counsellors might choose to use their lunch hours or evening time or time owed for work they have already done that was outside their normal working hours.

5 In some situations, individual practitioners have called upon the Advisory Service to Institutions, a sub-committee of the Association for Student Counselling. The Advisory Service attempts to advise both individuals and institutions on the work of counselling services. Their advice, support, help and sometimes intervention on such matters can be helpful.

6 Often, it may be just one person in the management structure who is blocking progress. Working out different ways of approaching the issue with this person might be beneficial.

7 The reality of restricted funding to departments might mean that there is no objection in principle to funding consultancy but that there is no money available. In these circumstances counsellors have engaged in income-generating activities (e.g. running courses) to supplement their office budgets in order that they determine the relative merits of different expenditure.

In summation, personal consultancy/supervision is recognised as being a crucial component in the counsellor's capacity to work effectively, humanely and efficiently. Having a personal consultant enables the counsellor to reflect systematically upon their practice, to discuss the more troubling cases and to feel supported in their task of being on the 'emotional front-line'.

Inevitably, seeing a consultant once a week will not always be enough to sustain the counsellor's morale and sense of well-being. As has been noted earlier in the book, student counsellors, because of their unique work within the college system, can come to feel quite isolated and alone. Also, counsellors can face particularly difficult circumstances when they are experiencing stress and difficulties within their own lives and having to contend with those of their clients.

Counsellors need to take good care of themselves in other ways as well as supervision. These might include periods of time in personal therapy, attending training courses, maintaining contact with other counselling colleagues, attending regional meetings of counsellors, paying attention to personal needs, pursuing other interests and activities, maintaining social relationships and so on.

The dangers of not taking care of themselves are considerable and can include susceptibility to physical illnesses, depression, resentment of clients, paranoid feelings towards the employers and employing institution and a general deterioration of relationships with colleagues with a consequent loss of good-will.

To look after others, counsellors have to look after themselves.

CLIENT DEMAND

As was mentioned in Chapter 1, the first student counsellors were appointed in further and higher education during the early 1960s. A spread of new appointments occurred during the following fifteen years and by the late 1970s several services had grown to the size of three full-time counsellors plus reception support.

In all these years the client demand, from students and staff, had been growing steadily. However, during the mid-1980s, following an analysis of different counselling service annual reports, members of the Association for Student Counselling realised that client demand was expanding rapidly and beginning to exceed supply. Waiting lists began to appear for the first time. Within the last few years it seems as if waiting lists have become standard in most student counselling services, though obviously not desirable.

Both individual students and staff require, from time to time, individual care and recognition. The recent rapid expansion in the student population and the increased pressures on academic staff mean that much less tutorial time is spent (individually or with small groups) with students. The counsellor is one of the few staff whose role is geared towards working with individuals on matters meaningful to their lives.

The task of counselling is directly related to fostering personal learning and as such, has a strong educative role. We predict that counsellors in the next few years are going to come under increasing pressures from their employers to see more students, more quickly, for less time. At worst the task they perform will be little understood and will not be valued by senior staff.

Notwithstanding the above, the groundswell of appreciation for counselling as a potent method of self-help is being expressed by students and staff alike. Counsellors will need to try to deal with these demands creatively and also continue to demonstrate the benefits of counselling to the institution.

Counselling, as a professional activity within education, has certainly more than come of age in the UK. But what of the future?

THE FUTURE

Given the scenario of larger student populations, a more complex range of academic courses than ever before, a broader student mix and increased client need, it is imperative that counselling services move towards having substantially improved resourcing. Additional staff and financial resources will enable counsellors to deploy their preventative and developmental skills with individuals and with groups, with students and with staff right across the college. This pattern of development has already occurred in the USA, Canada, Australia and New Zealand.

Several specific issues are likely to have particular significance and will demand some considerable professional attention in the next few years. We have briefly outlined three such arenas below.

International developments

The first involves the development of internationalism, in its many forms. The anticipated effects of European legislation relating to counsellors and psychotherapists are already causing considerable concern to various professional bodies and individual practitioners in the UK. Professional qualifications and licences to practice may become much harder to get and to maintain. Also, within Europe, an increasing number of student exchanges are occurring, thus bringing the need for student counsellors to have enhanced knowledge of different educational systems and knowledge of local sources of help for students in other countries.

The Association of European Vice-Chancellors and Principals of Universities in association with the International Round Table for the Advancement of Counselling has recently held a conference on this very theme. It has recognised the wide disparity of counsellor provision in the various member states and is keen to develop different initiatives in this regard.

The demands of world politics, trade and education mean that student counsellors will increasingly be exposed to students from countries all over the world. They will need to extend their skills, knowledge and expertise to be able to respond helpfully to increasingly culturally diverse student populations.

The tension between client need and institutional need

A second issue that may prove demanding upon student counsellors in the near future is that of the exact nature of their work, as determined by themselves on the one hand and by their employers on the other. The point has already been made in this book that student populations have become more varied during the last decade. Not only have student numbers increased but so have types of students attending. Also, the recent political socio-economic climate has had considerable effects. Changes in student funding and decreased opportunities for casual employment have combined to create a rather more stressed environment in which students now have to learn. The above interplay of factors has meant that student counsellors will increasingly be challenged by a range of clients presenting serious personal issues requiring help.

Also, at a national level, existing psychiatric services are being substantially decreased in favour of a policy of care in the community. Counsellors, who historically would have referred some clients for psychiatric assessment and help (and of course still need to do so) are now being referred student clients by psychiatrists for counselling.

Client demand for long-term counselling, therefore, is likely to increase. Student counsellors as a body are now a very experienced and skilled group of mental health professionals. They are well positioned to provide therapeutic services to the further and higher education community.

By contrast, the pressure of student numbers, the under-resourcing of counselling services and the wider remit of working in educational settings will constitute an intensification of the counsellor's dilemma of how best and most effectively to devote their time and scarce resources. To work in more depth with individuals who are seriously troubled or to provide minimal support for more students? To work only as a therapist or to work as a staff trainer and educator? To run more groups specifically geared to mental health or to stimulate group-work on developmental courses?

The above propositions, of necessity, have been presented as bald choices. The reality of these issues in coming years is more likely to be one of careful consideration and professional debate based upon systematic reflections on the work. It is likely that counsellors will seek to achieve a creative balance between these opposing tensions and, importantly, they will have to do so in relation to their employers and to emerging trends in further and higher education.

The changing structure of academic life and increased needs for educational guidance

Currently, there is pressure on institutions of higher education to move to a semester-based system of learning rather than academic terms. All parts of courses will be designed as modules and students will have to score a specific number of credits, accumulated through modules, to acquire their final qualifications. Certain modules are likely to be compulsory and others will be available to student choice. It is anticipated that the existing government policy of increasing student numbers will continue until at least the end of the century. National considerations are also under way to explore the possibility of 'fast-track' two-year degrees which will require a forty-five-week teaching year (as opposed to the present thirty to thirty-five weeks).

Also, to accommodate increased throughput of students, the traditional summer vacation period is being considered as a further opportunity for academic work, with the result that students may study in the first and third semesters and not during the second one (approximately April to June). The traditional structure of the academic year may soon disappear.

All of the above changes, if they come to fruition, will mean that students have to make a much greater range of choices than ever before as to what and when they study and what the implications of these choices will be for future careers. The emergence of an increased demand for tutorial and subject 'guidance' will inevitably impact upon counselling services. The American model of student counselling involves and includes guidance activities (advice and information provision on course choice) in addition to the activity of counselling that has been discussed in this book. Will student counsellors become involved in these developments? How? As subject advisers, or as co-ordinators of guidance tutors in departments or as trainers to such personnel in interviewing procedures and the enabling of informal choice? Again, dependent upon national developments, these policies may have considerable effects upon the future role of student counselling.

Counsellors are uniquely positioned to work with anyone in the institution. They have skills of working with student groups and they can facilitate staff development. All these activities and more substantiate a view of counsellors as persons who contribute to the smooth and humane running of large educational establishments. Counsellors believe that if the psychological and emotional needs of students and staff are attended to, then they are better able to function academically and creatively. Various research studies support their view that the student counsellor has a significant part to play in this overall educational endeavour.

We hope that the next decade will see institutional recognition of the value of counselling provision and that services will be appropriately resourced to fulfil the aims and objectives of their work. We have no doubt that counsellors, on their part, will devote themselves conscientiously and professionally to the demands that are likely to face them in the coming years and will continue to seek to explore the many challenges posed by therapeutic educational work in college settings. In short, student counsellors remain professionally committed to enabling others to learn to live and live to learn.

Further Reading

Bramley, W. (1979) *Group Tutoring: Concepts and Case Studies*, London: Kogan Page.

Erikson, E. H. (1980) *Identity and the Life Cycle*, New York: Norton & Collins.

Golan, N. (1981) *Passing Through Transitions*, New York: The Free Press.

Grayson, P. A. and Cauley, K. (1989) *College Psychotherapy*, New York: Guildford Press.

Kennedy, E. (1977) *On Becoming a Counsellor*, Dublin: Gill & Macmillan.

Newsome, A., Thorne, B. and Wylde, K. (1973) *Student Counselling in Practice*, London: Hodder & Stoughton.

Salzberger-Wittenberg, I., Henry, G. and Osborne, E. (1987) *The Emotional Experience of Learning and Teaching*, London: Routledge.

Wheeler, S. and Birtle, J. (1993) *The Handbook for Personal Tutors*, Buckingham: SRHE and Open University Press.

Training Resources

COUNSELLING SKILLS COURSES

Inskipp, F. (1986) *The Trainer's Handbook*, Cambridge: National Extension College.

Woolfe, R. (1989) *Counselling Skills*, Edinburgh: Scottish Health Education Group.

COURSES ON TUTORING, GROUP-WORK AND RESIDENTIAL TUTORING

Bramley, W. (1979) *Group Tutoring: Concepts and Case Studies*, London: Kogan Page.

Lago, C. O. and Shipton, G. A. (1994) *Personal Tutoring in Action: A Handbook for those in Student Support Roles*, Sheffield: University of Sheffield Staff Development Unit.

Rickenson, B. (1991) *Video on Personal Tutoring*, Birmingham: University of Birmingham AVA Unit.

WORK WITH INTERNATIONAL STUDENTS

Lago, C. O. (1990) *Working with Overseas Students: A Staff Development Training Manual*, Huddersfield: British Council and Huddersfield University.

United Kingdom Council for Overseas Student Affairs (1990) *The UKCOSA Manual*, London: UKCOSA.

STRESS MANAGEMENT COURSES

Patel, C. (1989) *The Complete Guide to Stress Management*, London: MacDonald & Co.

References

CHAPTER 1

Barkham, M. (1993) 'Counselling for brief periods', in *Questions and Answers on Counselling in Action*, London: Sage.

Dryden, W. (ed.) (1984) *Individual Therapy in Britain*, London: Harper & Row.

Karasu T. *et al*. (1984) *The Psychological Therapies*, Washington, DC: American Psychiatric Press.

Milner, P. (1974) *Counselling in Education*, London: J. M. Dent & Sons.

Newsome, A., Thorne, B. and Wylde, K. (1973) *Student Counselling in Practice*, London: Hodder & Stoughton.

Noonan, E. (1983) *Counselling Young People*, London: Methuen.

Ratigan, B. (1989) 'Counselling in higher education', in D. Charles-Edwards, W. Dryden and R. Woolfe (eds), *Handbook of Counselling in Britain*, London: Tavistock/Routledge.

Swainson, M. (1977) *Spirit of Counsel*, Sudbury: Neville Spearman.

CHAPTER 2

Fisher, S. (1989) *Homesickness, Cognition and Health*, Hove and London: Lawrence Erlbaum Associates.

Golan, N. (1981) *Passing Through Transitions*, New York: The Free Press.

Jordan, J. V., Stiver, J. B., Kaplan, A. G., Miller, J. B. and Surrey, J. L. (1991) *Women's Growth in Connection: Writings from the Stone Center*, New York: Guildford Press.

Noonan, E. (1986) 'The impact of the institution on psychotherapy', *Psychoanalytic Psychotherapy*, vol. 2, no. 2, pp. 126–7.

On Listening and Learning

CHAPTER 3

Bell, E., Dryden, W., Noonan, E. and Thorne, B. (1992) *A Guide to Recognizing Best Practice in Counselling*, Rugby: Association for Student Counselling.
Fisher, S. (1989) *Homesickness, Cognition and Health*, Hove and London: Lawrence Erlbaum Associates.

CHAPTER 5

D'Ardenne, P. and Mahtani, A. (1989) *Transcultural Counselling in Action*, London: Sage.
Hall, E. T. (1959) *The Silent Language*, New York: Anchor Press/Doubleday.
—— (1966) *The Hidden Dimension*, New York: Anchor Press/Doubleday.
Hofstede, G. (1980) *Culture's Consequences: International Differences in Work-Related Values*, Beverly Hills: Sage Publications.
Hughes, B. (1991) *Feeling at Home*, British Council booklet.
Lago, C. O. (1990) *Working with Overseas Students: A Staff Development Training Manual*, Huddersfield: British Council and Huddersfield University.
—— (1992) 'Some complexities in counselling international students', *Journal of International Education*, vol. 3, no. 1 (March).
—— and Thompson, J. (1989) 'Counselling and race', in D. Charles-Edwards, W. Dryden and R. Woolfe (eds), *Handbook of Counselling in Britain*, London: Tavistock/Routledge.
Williams, R. (1983) *Keywords: A Vocabulary of Culture and Society*, London: Flamingo.

CHAPTER 6

Gleik, J. (1988) *Chaos*, London: Heinemann.

CHAPTER 7

Dryden, W. (1978) 'Examination anxiety: what the student counsellor can do', *British Journal of Guidance and Counselling*, vol. 6, no. 2 (July).

CHAPTER 8

Inskipp, F. (1986) *The Trainer's Handbook*, Cambridge: National Extension College.

Index